Islam

Islam as a religion and a way of life guides millions of people around the world and has a significant impact on worldly affairs. To many Muslims, however, a philosophical understanding or assessment of Islamic belief is seen as a feeble and religiously inappropriate human attempt to understand matters that are beyond rational comprehension. *Islam: A Contemporary Philosophical Investigation* explores this issue in detail, by guiding readers through a careful study of the relationship between faith and reason in Islam. In particular, it pays close attention to religious objections to philosophizing about Islam, arguments for and against Islamic belief, and the rationality of Islamic belief in light of contemporary philosophical issues, such as problems of religious diversity, evil and religious doubt.

This text is appropriate for upper-level undergraduates and graduate students seeking an objective, philosophical introduction to Islam, a subject of increasing interest in classrooms around the world.

Imran Aijaz is an Associate Professor of Philosophy at the University of Michigan-Dearborn, USA.

Investigating Philosophy of Religion
Series editors: Chad Meister, *Bethel College*
Charles Taliaferro, *St. Olaf College*

This is a series of interfaith texts that philosophically engage with the major world religions in light of central issues they are currently facing. Each work is an original contribution by a leading scholar from that religious tradition and incorporates the latest developments in scholarship in the field. The texts are written for students, scholars, and all those who want a fairly detailed but concise overview of the central issues in contemporary philosophy of religion from the perspective of the major world religions.

Available

Judaism
A Contemporary Philosophical Investigation
Lenn E. Goodman

Buddhism
A Contemporary Philosophical Investigation
David Burton

Islam
A Contemporary Philosophical Investigation
Imran Aijaz

Forthcoming

Hinduism
A Contemporary Philosophical Investigation
Shyam Ranganathan

Daoism
A Contemporary Philosophical Investigation
Livia Kohn

Confucianism
A Contemporary Philosophical Investigation
Xinzhong Yao

For more information about this series, please visit: https://www.routledge.com/Investigating-Philosophy-of-Religion/book-series/IPR

Islam
A Contemporary Philosophical Investigation

Imran Aijaz

LONDON AND NEW YORK

First published 2018
by Routledge
2 Park Square, Milton Park, Abingdon, Oxon OX14 4RN

and by Routledge
711 Third Avenue, New York, NY 10017

Routledge is an imprint of the Taylor & Francis Group, an informa business

© 2018 Imran Aijaz

The right of Imran Aijaz to be identified as author of this work has been asserted by him in accordance with sections 77 and 78 of the Copyright, Designs and Patents Act 1988.

All rights reserved. No part of this book may be reprinted or reproduced or utilised in any form or by any electronic, mechanical, or other means, now known or hereafter invented, including photocopying and recording, or in any information storage or retrieval system, without permission in writing from the publishers.

Trademark notice: Product or corporate names may be trademarks or registered trademarks, and are used only for identification and explanation without intent to infringe.

British Library Cataloguing-in-Publication Data
A catalogue record for this book is available from the British Library

Library of Congress Cataloging-in-Publication Data
A catalog record for this book has been requested

ISBN: 978-1-138-91021-8 (hbk)
ISBN: 978-1-138-91022-5 (pbk)
ISBN: 978-1-315-69353-8 (ebk)

Typeset in Times New Roman
by codeMantra

Contents

	Acknowledgments	vi
	Preface	vii
1	Can Islam be investigated philosophically?	1
2	Classical traditionalist fideism in Islam	14
3	Classical scholastic fideism in Islam	35
4	Contemporary fideism in Islam	76
5	Rationalist arguments for Islamic belief	100
6	Religious doubt, Islamic faith and the Skeptical Muslim	112
	Index	127

Acknowledgments

Working on this book and bringing it into its current form has been a prolonged and difficult undertaking, one which could not have been completed without the help, advice and encouragement of several people. I have greatly benefited from discussions of my work with Zain Ali, Ben Miller, John Bishop, Greg Dawes, Oliver Leaman, Robert McKim and Markus Weidler; to all these people, I offer my thanks. I am also grateful to the anonymous reviewer of my manuscript for reading through it and for offering some suggestions that allowed me to make improvements. I am indebted to the series editors, Chad Meister and Charles Taliaferro, for their constant support, patience and understanding in seeing this project to its completion, despite unforeseen setbacks. I would also like to thank the staff at Routledge for their patience and help in the production of this book.

I owe a special debt of gratitude to my family. To my parents, I owe more than I could possibly say for the sacrifices they made to ensure that I had a good education. It is thanks to them that I can appreciate the force behind the question posed in the Islamic Scripture: "Say, 'Are those equal, those who know and those who do not know?'" (Qur'an 39:9). Last, but certainly not least, I am grateful to my wife, Brennan, for her love, care and support during my work on this project. In countless instances, I have found her views on things to be much wiser than what I, as a philosopher, had to offer: "She speaks with wisdom, and faithful instruction is on her tongue" (Proverbs 31:26).

Preface

In this book, I seek to provide a contemporary philosophical investigation of Islam. While philosophers continue to disagree about the precise definition of 'philosophy', few would deny the central role that arguments play in the discipline. Here is how Richard Popkin emphasizes this role in his definition of philosophy:

> Philosophy is the attempt to give an account of what is true and what is important, based on a rational assessment of evidence and arguments rather than myth, tradition, bald assertion, oracular utterances, local custom, or mere prejudice.[1]

As Popkin explains, this understanding of philosophy can be traced back to the Greeks around the 5th century BCE.[2] In conducting a philosophical investigation of Islam, it is this classic conception of philosophy that I will be operating under. In doing so, I will be engaged in an exercise that is part of the branch of philosophy known as the Philosophy of Religion, which David Stewart helpfully defines as follows:

> Philosophy of religion is not a systematic statement of religious beliefs (which would be theology or dogmatics) but a second-order activity focused on the fundamental issues of a given religion. Christians, for example, talk a lot about God, but what is the evidence that God exists? If God's existence can be proved, how does one go about it? And if God exists, how can one account for the presence of evil in the world? Such questions are philosophical in nature, and the philosopher of religion will not be content to let such questions go unexamined. The task of philosophy of religion, at least as it is conceived of in the West, is to submit claims such as those made by religions to a thoroughgoing rational investigation.[3]

It is this 'second-order' aspect of Philosophy of Religion that distinguishes it from some other approaches to religion, such as theology or apologetics, where the truth of religious beliefs (e.g., beliefs about the existence of God,

viii   *Preface*

the authority of revelation, etc.) is simply presupposed prior to an inquiry. In philosophically investigating Islam, I am interested in rationally examining the truth of Islamic belief through evidence and argument.

But *why* philosophically investigate Islam? A variety of answers can be given to this question. Here is one answer that I think is compelling. The Islamic religion offers us an account of reality that is supposed to be very important. This account is based on several theological propositions, such as 'Allah exists', 'There is no god other than Allah', 'Muhammad is Allah's Prophet', etc. Because they *believe* such theological propositions to be true, Muslims engage in a variety of religious *practices* that are connected to these beliefs, such as prayer, fasting, pilgrimage to Mecca and so on. To make this point is simply to draw attention to a specifically religious instance of the more general fact that there is a connection between belief and action. Beliefs typically influence the actions that we take; they are, as Frank Ramsey put it using his famous metaphor, "maps by which we steer."[4] If I hold the belief that p, then I will typically employ that belief in my practical reasoning towards any action where whether it is the case that p is relevant and salient. For instance, my belief that I am teaching a class at the university this afternoon will be incorporated into my practical reasoning towards whether I need to visit the university campus today. Virtually all Muslim thinkers accept this point, certainly insofar as it applies to Islamic belief and practice. Indeed, many of them explain Islamic commitment as involving a complete 'way of life'. For instance, the famous Pakistani Muslim thinker Sayyid Abu A'la Maududi succinctly explains the connection between Islamic belief and practice as follows:

> The main characteristic of Islamic ideology is that it does not acknowledge a conflict; not even a slight separation between spiritual life and mundane life. It does not confine itself merely to purifying the spiritual and the moral life of man in the limited sense of the word. Its scope extends to the entire aspects of life.[5]

It is obvious that Islamic practice has a significant impact on worldly affairs. To consider just a few examples, traditional Muslims will typically consume meat that is only *halal* (Islamically permissible); they will avoid the consumption of pork and alcohol; they will refrain from getting into financial matters where interest is involved; and, they will slaughter millions of animals each year during *Eid al-Adha* (The 'Festival of Sacrifice'). Many of these Islamic practices are also open to *moral* evaluation. For instance, several people, including some Muslims, have raised ethical concerns about the mass slaughter of animals for *Eid al-Adha*.[6] Given the practical and ethical import of Islamic practice and the fact that it can be traced back to Islamic belief, it seems clear that the truth or falsity of such belief is a crucial matter. This is where a philosophical investigation of Islam can play an important role. While it is laudable for any person to show interest in philosophical investigations of

Islam, it is especially important for Muslims to take these seriously. After all, Muslims are the ones who are engaged in Islamic practice, which is motivated and animated by Islamic belief, and it is such belief that will be the focus of scrutiny whenever Islam is subjected to a philosophical investigation.

My approach to a philosophical investigation of Islam in this book will proceed as follows. In Chapter 1 ('Can Islam be investigated philosophically?'), I note that what is called 'fideism' poses perhaps the most significant obstacle to those who want to offer the results of a philosophical investigation of Islam to the Muslim community. In essence, the view of the fideist emphasizes the acceptance of religious claims 'by faith' over reason. In the first chapter of the book, I provide a brief historical outline of the relationship between faith and reason in Islam. In doing so, I carve out some terms to delineate a number of different perspectives that Muslims have taken on the relationship between faith and reason. Under the rubric of what I call 'anti-rationalistic fideism', the view that revelation precedes reason in determining the truth of religious (Islamic) belief, there are two variants – 'traditionalist fideism' and 'scholastic fideism'. Both these variants of anti-rationalistic fideism begin with the claims of Islamic revelation as a given, prior to any sort of inquiry into religious matters. The difference between the two lies in the role and scope of reason in discussions about Islam. While the traditionalist fideists only allowed reason to be used minimally, if at all, in religious discussions, the scholastic fideists saw no problem in deploying rational argument in the service of defending Islamic belief. In Chapter 2 ('Classical traditionalist fideism in Islam'), I evaluate the plausibility of classical traditionalist fideism in Islam by looking at some of the arguments given by one of its most famous representatives – the Palestinian traditionalist Muwaffaq ad-Din b. Qudama (d. 1223). This is followed, in Chapter 3 ('Classical scholastic fideism in Islam'), by a substantive critical assessment of classical scholastic fideism in Islam as found in the works of Abu Hamid al-Ghazali (d. 1111). As I explain in that chapter, it is important to engage with al-Ghazali's arguments regarding philosophical speculation about religious matters, given that he is often heralded by Muslims as the great defender of Islamic orthodoxy who refuted philosophy. In Chapter 4 ('Contemporary fideism in Islam'), I turn my attention to some contemporary trends in Islamic fideistic thought as found in the writings of two fundamentalist Muslim thinkers – Sayyid Abu A'la Maududi (d. 1979) and Sayyid Qutb (d. 1966). These four chapters that focus on an understanding and evaluation of Islamic anti-rationalistic fideism constitute most of this book. In pointing this out to readers, I anticipate two concerns that may be raised. First, one might wonder why I am giving *so much* attention to fideism in Islam and, second, one might complain that an assessment of Islamic fideism isn't really a *philosophical* investigation of Islam. Let me reply to these two points in turn.

To the first point, I will simply reemphasize what was said earlier. Although a philosophical investigation of Islam is an important enterprise,

x *Preface*

many Muslims today are simply resistant to it. This force of this point is typically not appreciated by those who are not part of the Muslim community, but it is well known to contemporary Islamic philosophers. The late Islamic philosopher Fazlur Rahman, for instance, explains why, from his perspective, philosophy is important both in a general sense as well as for religion:

> Philosophy is ... a perennial intellectual need and has to be allowed to flourish both for its own sake and for the sake of other disciplines, since it inculcates a much-needed analytical-critical spirit and generates new ideas that become important intellectual tools for other sciences, not least for religion and theology. Therefore a people that deprives itself of philosophy necessarily exposes itself to starvation in terms of fresh ideas – in fact, it commits intellectual suicide.[7]

But he also notes that, since medieval times, "philosophy has been a disciplina non grata in the Muslim educational system throughout a large part of the Muslim world."[8] A large part of the Islamic opposition to philosophical investigations of Islam, as I have noted, comes from the Muslim adoption of fideism. A careful and sustained critical examination of Islamic fideism will therefore be invaluable in paving the way for Muslims to take philosophy and philosophical investigations of their faith seriously.

My reply to the second point is that it isn't at all clear an assessment of Islamic fideism does not constitute a philosophical investigation of Islam. As will be seen over the course of the chapters in which I evaluate Islamic fideism, all the Muslim fideists surveyed offer *arguments* for their views. It is tempting to see their efforts as amounting to philosophizing about Islamic belief, in the way that Al-Kindi (d. 873), the 'Philosopher of the Arabs', did in responding to opponents of philosophy:

> [F]or they must say that [the pursuit of philosophy] is either necessary or not necessary. If they say that it is necessary, then its pursuit is necessary for them. If, on the other hand, they say that it is not necessary, it is necessary for them ... to give a demonstration of this ... Pursuit of this acquisition is, therefore, required by their own tongues, and devotion to it is necessary for them.[9]

Some of the fideistic stances examined in this book, such as the one developed by al-Ghazali, are quite sophisticated and can be regarded as the adoption of a philosophical position on the relationship between faith and reason. As Richard Amesbury notes in his helpful survey of the topic, fideism may be seen as "denoting a particular *philosophical* account of faith's appropriate jurisdiction vis-a-vis that of reason."[10] Construed as a philosophical position, fideism may be investigated philosophically. Suppose, however, that neither fideism nor a critical assessment of it counts as something philosophical. It would still be the case that an evaluation of fideism is important for a philosophical investigation of

Islam, as mentioned earlier. In this work, I shall simply assume that my critique of Islamic fideism does not amount to a philosophical investigation of Islam, even though I think a case can be made for thinking otherwise.[11]

In Chapter 5 ('Rationalist arguments for Islamic belief'), the penultimate chapter of the book, I turn my attention to a philosophical investigation of Islamic belief, having argued against fideistic criticisms of such an endeavor in the previous chapters. Specifically, I consider the force of some standard rationalist arguments that Muslims have given to support the truth of Islamic belief. These are mainly arguments for the existence of God and the Prophethood of Muhammad. I argue that these arguments fail to provide rational support for Islamic belief. In this chapter, I also sketch out an outline of what a successful rationalist vindication of Islamic belief would require. In the final chapter of the book, Chapter 6 ('Religious doubt, Islamic faith and The Skeptical Muslim'), I defend the view that a person who harbors religious doubts about Islamic belief can nevertheless embrace a skeptical kind of faith. In this chapter, I respond to a number of arguments that have been given against the viability of such a position as well as consider how a positive case may be developed for seeing religious doubt as a virtue.

One final remark is in order before we get going with the task at hand. In a general sense, a philosophical investigation of Islam is surely a monumental endeavor. On this interpretation, to philosophically investigate Islam would require a lengthy inquiry into the plausibility of Islamic belief, relying on several important disciplines such as theology, philosophy, history, science and so on. Furthermore, such an immense undertaking could not be done without a collective effort on the part of several individuals. My discussion in this book should be seen as a small and humble contribution to this undertaking; it consists of one person attempting to philosophically think his way through his religious tradition. By no means does my work in this book constitute a comprehensive philosophical assessment of the Islamic religion.

Imran Aijaz
Michigan, 2018

Notes

1 Richard Popkin, *The Pimlico History of Western Philosophy*, (London: Pimlico, 1999), p. 1.
2 Ibid.
3 David Stewart, *Exploring the Philosophy of Religion*, (Englewood Cliffs, NJ: Prentice-Hall Inc., 1980), p. 6.
4 Frank Plumpton Ramsey, *The Foundation of Mathematics and Other Logical Essays*, R. B. Braithwaite ed., (London: Routledge, 1931), p. 238.
5 A. A. Maududi, *Islamic Way of Life*, (Scribe Digital, 2012), p. 1.
6 See PETA's 'Animal Sacrifice: Not Needed at Any Time', www.peta.org/blog/animal-sacrifice-needed-eid-time/ and Tariq Ramadan, 'Eid al Adha: Animal Cruelty Contradicts the Spirit of Islam', www.abc.net.au/religion/articles/2015/09/24/4318680.htm for some discussion regarding the ethical aspects of this Islamic practice.

xii *Preface*

7 Fazlur Rahman, *Islam and Modernity*, (Chicago: University of Chicago Press, 1984), pp. 157–158.
8 Ibid., p. 157.
9 Al-Kindi, 'On First Philosophy', trans. Alfred L. Ivry, *Al-Kindi's Metaphysics*, (State University of New York Press, 1974), p. 59.
10 Richard Amesbury, 'Fideism', The Stanford Encyclopedia of Philosophy (Winter 2016 Edition), Edward N. Zalta (ed.), https://plato.stanford.edu/archives/win2016/entries/fideism/. Italics mine.
11 This particular issue does not have a significant bearing on my discussion in this book.

1 Can Islam be investigated philosophically?

1. Fideism as an obstacle to a philosophical investigation of Islam

"It should be known," wrote the 14th-century Tunisian polymath, Ibn Khaldun, in his *Prolegomena* (*Muqaddimah*), "that the [opinion] the [philosophers] hold is wrong in all its aspects."[1] In drawing up his list of the sacred and profane sciences in the sixth chapter of this work, he offers a summary refutation of philosophy that makes several points about the inadequacy of the discipline. Here is a specimen of his refutation:

> The great philosopher Plato said that no certainty can be achieved with regard to the Divine, and one can state about the Divine only what is most suitable and proper that is, conjectures. If, after all the toil and trouble, we find only conjectures, the (conjectures) that we had at the beginning may as well suffice us. What use, then, do these sciences and the pursuit of them have? We want certainty about the *existentia* that are beyond sensual perception while, in their (philosophy), (those conjectures) are the limit that human thinking can reach.[2]

Ibn Khaldun's dismissal of philosophy provides a fairly accurate representation of the prevailing Muslim attitude towards it today, about six and a half centuries after he penned his criticisms. Any attempt to investigate Islam philosophically runs the risk of being met with skepticism and resistance from Muslims who are unsympathetic, if not downright opposed, to philosophical inquiry into their faith. Philosophy is seen as religiously inappropriate, as misguided, as a source of confusion and error, as a feeble human attempt to understand matters that are and always will be beyond rational comprehension (at least during our early existence), etc. Such reasons principally stem from a more basic commitment to *fideism*, which the contemporary Islamic philosopher Shabbir Akhtar defines as "the theological doctrine according to which faith does not stand in need of rational justification; faith is indeed, in religious domains, the arbiter of reason and its pretensions."[3]

2 Can Islam be investigated?

As I have noted in the Preface, it is important for contemporary Muslims to take philosophical investigations of their faith seriously and to engage with them. If, however, fideism does indeed have a legitimate basis in Islam, it is difficult to see how this can happen. A critical assessment of Islamic fideism will therefore be important in urging Muslims to give due consideration to philosophical investigations of Islam.

2. Faith and reason in Islam: a brief historical outline

Throughout the history of Western philosophy and its interaction with the Abrahamic religions, much has been said about the legitimacy, role and scope of philosophical reflection about religious matters. In this chapter, I will provide only a very brief historical outline of some key positions regarding the relationship between faith and reason that were adopted by Muslim thinkers throughout Islamic history. This outline will provide a useful framework for my subsequent discussion and assessment of Islamic fideism.

Within mainstream Sunni Islam, one can identify two broad stances on the relationship between faith and reason, which I shall call *anti-rationalistic fideism* and *theistic rationalism*. Anti-rationalistic fideism can be divided into two further stances, which I shall call *traditionalist fideism* and *scholastic fideism*. Let me explain these labels. By 'anti-rationalistic fideism', I shall mean the view that *revelation precedes reason in determining the truth of religious (Islamic) belief*. By contrast, I shall define 'theistic rationalism' as the view that *reason precedes revelation in determining the truth of religious (Islamic) belief*. Thus understood, anti-rationalistic fideism and theistic rationalism are distinct and mutually exclusive views; the truth of one entails the falsity of the other.

The difference between anti-rationalistic fideism and theistic rationalism can be helpfully clarified using Binyamin Abrahamov's distinction between 'rationalism' and 'rationality' in a theological context:

> [T]he term rationalism ... means the tendency to consider reason the principal device or one of the principal devices to reach the truth in religion, and the preference of reason to revelation and tradition in dealing with some theological matters, mainly when a conflict arises between them ... The term 'rationalism' must be distinguished from 'rationality' which means treating any issue by using reason, but without giving reason priority. Rationality turns to rationalism when reason is prior to revelation.[4]

Anti-rationalistic fideism is not, then, anti-rational but anti-rationalistic. Although he rejects the priority of reason over revelation, it remains an open question whether the anti-rationalistic fideist is interested in using reason in discussions about religious truth. Those anti-rationalistic fideists who showed little or no interest in reason when discussing the truth about religious matters I shall call adherents of 'traditionalist fideism', based on

Abrahamov's definition of 'traditionalists' as "those who regarded religious knowledge as deriving from the Revelation (the Qur'an), the Tradition (the Sunna) and the Consensus (*ijmā'*) and preferred these sources to reason in treating religious matters."[5] By contrast, the anti-rationalistic fideists who incorporated reason significantly into their discussions of the truth about religious matters I shall call adherents of 'scholastic fideism'.

The threads of thought that constitute traditionalist fideism in Islam can be found in the works of the four famous Imams of the Sunni tradition: Abu Hanifah (d. 767), Malik b. Anas (d. 795), al-Shafi'i (d. 820) and Ahmad Ibn Hanbal (d. 855), and, later, among those who would follow their juridical schools of law (*madhahib*). Of these four schools, those who followed Ibn Hanbal – the Hanabilah – showed perhaps the fiercest opposition to any sort of philosophical inquiry in relation to Islamic belief. For Ibn Hanbal, religious faith primarily involves submitting to religious authority. Attempts to systematically reason out religious doctrine in any way are prohibited:

> Whoever asserts that he does not approve of uncritical faith ... and that he will not follow others in matters of faith, that one has made a sinful utterance in the eyes of God and His Apostle (may God bless him and grant him salvation). By such an attitude he aims at the invalidation of tradition, the degrading of knowledge and *sunnah*. He is concerned only with subjective opinion, speculative theology (*kalām*), innovation and dissension.[6]

This basic view, formulated by Ibn Hanbal over a thousand years ago, is still dominant in Muslim societies today and is the cornerstone of Islamic 'orthodoxy'. As Wesley Williams observes, "[a]s the patron saint of the traditionalists, [Ibn Hanbal's] dogmatic views would eventually become the shibboleth of Sunni 'orthodoxy'."[7] Following Ibn Hanbal, several famous thinkers belonging to his school composed polemical treatises censuring speculative reasoning about religious matters and urging the faithful to adhere or return to his simple religious creed. As examples, we can mention 'Abd Allah al-Ansari al-Harawi's (d. 1088) *Condemnation of Speculative Theology and Its Advocates* (*Dhamm al-kalam wa-ahlih*),[8] Muwaffaq ad-Din b. Qudama's (d. 1223) *A Thesis on Prohibiting the Study of Works by the Partisans of Speculative Theology* (*Mas'ala fi tahrim an-nazar fi kutb ahl al-kalam*),[9] and Ibn Taymiyyah's (d. 1327) *Refutation of the Logicians* (*Al-Radd 'ala 'l-Mantiqiyin*).[10]

The roots of scholastic fideism go back to a group of early Muslim thinkers known as the Mu'tazilites, whose origins are obscure. According to the dominant traditional account, the reason that the Mu'tazilites were so called can be traced to the figure of al-Hasan al-Basri (d. 728), a famous and important Muslim thinker who debated several theological issues among a circle of scholars who had gathered in Basra, Iraq. One of the scholars of that circle was Wasil ibn Ata (d. 748), generally credited as being the founder of the Mu'tazilites, who eventually 'broke off' (*i'tazala*) from al-Hasan. It is supposedly to this act of 'withdrawal' that the label 'Mu'tazilites' is in

4 Can Islam be investigated?

reference to.[11] In all of their theological discussions, the starting point for the Mu'tazilites is reason as opposed to revelation. As D. Gimaret observes,

> [T]he Mu'tazilites are incontestably rationalists, in the true sense of the term, in that they consider that certain awarenesses [sic] are accessible to man by means of his intelligence alone, in the absence of, or prior to, any revelation.[12]

According to the Mu'tazilites, among the things that may be known by reason independently of revelation are the existence of God, various aspects of the Divine Nature and the truthfulness of Muhammad's Prophethood.[13] Essentially, on their view, the truth of Islamic theism can be known through reason alone. Consider, as an example to contrast the views of Ibn Hanbal with, what 'Abd al-Jabbar (d. 1025), one of the last great thinkers of the Mu'tazilite school, says in the opening of his *Book of the Five Fundamentals* (*Kitab al-Usul al-khamsa*):

1. **If it is asked**: What is the first duty that God imposes upon you? *Say to him*: Speculative reasoning (*al-nazar*) which leads to knowledge of God, because He is not known intuitively (*daruratan*) nor by the senses (*bi l-mushahada*). Thus, He must be known by reflection and speculation.[14]

For 'Abd al-Jabbar, then, acquiring knowledge of God through speculative reasoning is our first important duty. In explaining this duty, no appeal is made to sources of religious authority, for example, the Qur'an.

The Mu'tazilites were clearly adherents of theistic rationalism. Given that, on their view, reason precedes revelation in determining the truth about religious belief, they were certainly not anti-rationalistic fideists. In addition to prioritizing reason over revelation in theological discussions, the Mu'tazilites were known for applying reason to religious matters in a sustained and methodical fashion. As Fazlur Rahman notes, "the impulse to a *systematic thinking out* of dogma ... was certainly an activity which made them pursue their ratiocination further and further as time went on."[15] This systematic thinking out of dogma, which involved careful reasoning and argumentation, came to be known as '*Ilm al-kalam* (or just *kalam*) – the science of 'speculative theology', roughly translated.[16] Although the origins of *kalam* are closely associated with the rise of the Mu'tazilites in the 8th century CE, its more definite and classical form would emerge two centuries later.

Since the anti-rationalistic fideism of the Hanabilah and the theistic rationalism of the Mu'tazilites represent two incompatible positions, it is not surprising that the two groups were constantly at loggerheads with each other. The height of the conflict between these two groups is often identified with the imprisonment of Ibn Hanbal himself under the rule of the Caliph al-Ma'mun (d. 833), who, as a sympathizer of Mu'tazilite theology, became a public advocate of the Mu'tazilite cause.[17] Between the years of 827 and 833, al-Ma'mun proclaimed the thesis of the 'created' Qur'an – one of the central doctrines of the Mu'tazilites – as official state doctrine across the empire.[18] It was Ibn Hanbal's defiance and opposition to the Mu'tazilite edict during this period and the following few years, which came to be known as the years of the Inquisition (*Mihna*), that saw him imprisoned. When al-Mutawakkil (d. 861) ascended to power in 847 as the new Caliph, however, the *Mihna* came to an end, the Mu'tazilites fell out of political favor and Ibn Hanbal emerged as the triumphant hero of orthodox Islam who, despite his persecution, had withstood the heresies of the Mu'tazilites.[19]

By around the middle of the 9th century CE, the dogmatic position of Ibn Hanbal had essentially integrated itself into, and became a representation of, Islamic orthodoxy, while the Mu'tazilites had become isolated and exercised little influence over the then prevalent theological discussions. As W. Montgomery Watt explains,

> With the abandonment of the policy of the 'inquisition' about 850 the caliphal government became pro-Sunnite, and what has been called the consolidation of Sunnism followed ... The Mu'tazilites had in fact become a group of academic theologians who had retired to an ivory tower remote from the tensions and pressures of ordinary life.[20]

Approximately half a century after the Mu'tazilite *Mihna* came to an end, another significantly influential theological position emerged in the works of Abu-l-Hasan al-Ash'ari (d. 935), whom Watt calls "one of the outstanding figures in the history of Islamic theology."[21] What makes al-Ash'ari such an important figure in Islamic history is that he was one of the first thinkers who attempted to charter a course between the Scylla of traditionalist fideism, as typified by the Hanabilah, and the Charybdis of Mu'tazilite rationalism. Originally a Mu'tazilite, al-Ash'ari was a student of the head of the Mu'tazilite school in the Iraqi city of Basra, al-Juba'i (d. 915), and, being a Mu'tazilite, was a student of *kalam*.

Because of the decline of interest in Mu'tazilite theology during the time of al-Ash'ari, it is not surprising that he "saw that Mu'tazilism in general was becoming increasingly irrelevant to the contemporary situation."[22] Tradition has it, however, that it was not merely an awareness of this fact, but a series of dreams during the month of Ramadan that prompted al-Ash'ari to defect from the Mu'tazilites.[23] In one of these dreams, the Prophet Muhammad appeared to him and told him to "give [his] support to the opinions related on [the Prophet's] authority, for they are the reality."[24] For a period of time following this dream, al-Ash'ari abandoned *kalam* and devoted himself diligently to the study of the Qur'an and the *Sunnah*.[25] Later, the Prophet appeared to him in the final of a series of dreams and asked what al-Ash'ari had done to fulfill the command bestowed upon him, to which the latter replied that he had given up *kalam* and confined himself to studying the Qur'an and the *Sunnah*. The Prophet's reply to al-Ash'ari was that this

6   *Can Islam be investigated?*

was not was he commanded him to do.[26] That is, the Prophet had commanded al-Ash'ari to take seriously religious doctrines that were related on his authority, but not to abandon the rational methods of *kalam*.[27]

Al-Ash'ari's abandonment of Mu'tazilite thought marked a turning point in the debate between the traditionalist fideists and the theistic rationalists in the Muslim community. As Watt explains, "on the basis of this conception [as conveyed to him by the Prophet in the final dream] al-Ash'ari worked out his new theological position, which may be described as the support of revelation by reason."[28] Specifically, on al-Ash'ari's new position, revelation precedes reason in determining the truth about religious belief. It is therefore still within the boundaries of anti-rationalistic fideism, but is not to be identified with traditionalist fideism. In his *The Elucidation of Islam's Foundations* (*Al-Ibanah 'An Usul Ad-Diyanah*), which was written after his defection from the Mu'tazilites, al-Ash'ari makes it clear that he no longer gives them his allegiance; they are, he avers, "deviators from the truth."[29] To be precise, there are ten particular doctrines of Islam on which the Mu'tazilites "dissent from the Book [the Qur'ān], and the *sunnah*, and that upon which the Prophet and his Companions take their stand and upon which the Community [of Muslims] have unanimously agreed."[30]

In *Al-Ibanah*, not only does al-Ash'ari declare what the starting point for theological discussion should be, but he also states where his newfound allegiance has been placed:

> The belief we hold and the religion we follow are holding fast to the Book of our Lord ..., to the *sunnah* of our Prophet, and to the traditions related on the authority of the Companions and the Successors and the *imāms* of the [*hadith*]; – to that we hold firmly, professing what Abū 'Abdallāh Ahmad ibn Muhammad ibn Hanbal professed, and avoiding him who dissents from this belief, because he is the excellent *imām* and the perfect leader, through whom God declared the truth, removed error, manifested the modes of action, and overcame the innovation of the innovators, the deviation of the deviators, and the skepticism of the skeptics. The mercy of God be upon him, – for he is an eminent *imām* and an exalted, honored friend, – and upon all the other *imāms* of Islam![31]

The profession of doctrine here is virtually identical to that of the traditionalist fideists, such as the Hanabilah. Indeed, al-Ash'ari makes it explicit that what he states was professed by Ibn Hanbal himself and goes on to praise him. With respect to the *starting point* for theological discussion, then, al-Ash'ari's new position is in agreement with that of the traditionalist fideists. Where there is a marked difference between the two, however, is in the *approach* taken in defending religious doctrine. In contrast to the Hanabilah and other traditionalist fideists, who would typically be content in responding to their opponents by merely appealing to religious authority, al-Ash'ari, not finding any objection to the methods of *kalam*, employed rational proofs and arguments to defend the traditionalists' creed.

Can Islam be investigated? 7

Whereas the traditionalists would often be content simply to quote verses from the Qur'an to prove a point, al-Ash'ari would cite a Qur'anic verse, as he does in *Al-Ibanah*, but would "[place] the verse in a setting of rational conceptions."[32] This framework can also be seen in his work *Highlights of the Polemic against Deviators and Innovators (Kitab Al-Luma' Fi'l-Radd 'Ala Ahl Al-Zaigh wa'l-Bida')*,[33] a work also authored after his defection and one which he describes as a "compendious book which ... [contains] a summary exposition of the arguments which elucidate what is true and refute what is vain and empty assertion."[34] For an example that clearly illustrates al-Ash'ari's post-Mu'tazilite theological framework, we can look at his discussion of the existence of God in section one of *Al-Luma'*. After first stating the question, 'What is the proof that creation has a maker who made it and a governor who wisely ordered it?', al-Ash'ari answers thus: "The proof of that is that the completely mature man was originally semen, then a clot, then a small lump, then flesh and bone and blood."[35] His preliminary answer is essentially Qur'anic, since this is more or less a quotation from the Qur'an.[36] But al-Ash'ari does not stop here. He proceeds to provide a rational elaboration and justification of this Qur'anic verse:

Now we know very well that [man] did not translate himself from state to state. For we see that at the peak of his physical and mental maturity he is unable to produce hearing and sight for himself, or to create a bodily member for himself. That proves that he is even more incapable of doing that when he was weak and imperfect. For if he can do a thing when he is imperfect, a fortiori he can do it when he is mature; and if he cannot do a thing when he is mature, a fortiori he is incapable of it when he is imperfect. From seeing him a baby, then a youth, then a man in the prime of life, then an old man, we know very well that he does not translate himself from youth to old age and decrepitude. For even though a man strain to rid himself of old age and decrepitude and to restore himself to his youthful condition, he cannot do it. So what we have said proves that it is not he who translates himself from state to state and governs his every condition: for his translation from state to state without a translator is impossible.[37]

To further support his reasoning inspired by the Qur'an, he continues to argue as follows:

An example which makes that clear is the fact that cotton cannot change into spun thread and woven cloth without weaver or craftsman or supervisor. If a man selected some cotton and then waited for it to become spun thread and woven cloth without craftsman or weaver, he would be beyond the pale of reason and abysmally ignorant. Likewise if a man went to a waste land and found there no castle already built, and waited for the clay to change into bricks which would join together without workman or builder, he would be witless. Now if the change of semen to

8   *Can Islam be investigated?*

clot, then little lump, then flesh and blood and bone be an even greater marvel, it proves all the more forcibly that there is a maker who made the semen and translated it from state to state.[38]

So although al-Ash'ari addresses the question of God's existence by starting with the authority of revelation, as he does in his treatment of other theological issues, he freely utilizes *kalam* to provide a rational justification of what is contained in Scripture.

Al-Ash'ari's use of *kalam* does not, however, go as far as *questioning* the truth of what is plainly stated in revelation (i.e., the Qur'an). The rationalism of the Mu'tazilites, whom al-Ash'ari deserted, would lead them so far as to interpret seemingly anthropomorphic verses in the Qur'an, which mention, for instance, God's 'hand' or 'face', in an allegorical manner.[39] Such rationalism is, for al-Ash'ari, too excessive. When reason conflicts with revelation, it is reason that must submit to the authority of revelation. Thus, rather than interpret the anthropomorphic expressions in the Qur'an allegorically, such expressions, avers al-Ash'ari, should be accepted 'without asking how' (*bila kayfa*). As he writes,

> God is upon the throne ... He has two hands, *bila kayfa* ... and He has two eyes, *bila kayfa* ... and He has a face ... The Sunnites ... assert the existence of His hearing and sight; and they do not deny that those things belong to God, as the Mu'tazilah do.[40]

It is this theological approach of al-Ash'ari's that eventually came to be identified with the discipline of *kalam*. Prior to him, most Islamic thinkers understood *kalam* to mean theistic rationalism as practiced by the Mu'tazilites, which had no theological constraints or presuppositions. What al-Ash'ari demonstrated was that *kalam* need not be understood in this way, and that it can, in fact, be separated from theistic rationalism. One can be a proponent of *kalam* while rejecting theistic rationalism, by confining the rational methods of the former to the boundaries of Islamic doctrine.

This new way of understanding *kalam* eventually became dominant after al-Ash'ari. In his *Prolegomena*, Ibn Khaldun defines *kalam* as "a science that involves arguing with logical proofs in defense of the articles of faith and refuting innovators who deviate in their dogmas from the early Muslims and Muslim orthodoxy."[41] This understanding of *kalam* is clearly Ash'arite, since it takes the purpose of logical proofs to be in *service* of Islamic doctrine. Indeed, Ibn Khaldun identifies the perfection of *kalam* with al-Ash'ari. Referring to the Mu'tazilite Inquisition, he says:

> This caused orthodox people to rise in defense of the articles of faith with logical evidence and to push back the innovations. The leader of the speculative theologians, Abul-Hasan al-Ash'ari, took care of that. He mediated between the different approaches ... with the help of

Can Islam be investigated? 9

logical and traditional methods. He refuted the innovators in all these respects ... Thus, (al-Ash'ari's) approach was perfected and became one of the best speculative disciplines and religious sciences.[42]

In contemporary discussions when *kalam* is mentioned in a generic way, it is almost always the Ash'arite interpretation of it that is being referred to. Thus, F. E. Peters, for example, refers to *kalam* as 'dialectical theology', and, without qualification, writes that "dialectical theology in Islam resembled the Christians' 'sacred theology', which took the givens of revelation as its starting point and attempted to demonstrate dialectically the conclusions that flowed from them."[43] What Peters says here is correct only if one is referring to the Ash'arite understanding of *kalam* and not its earlier Mu'tazilite interpretation.

I shall take Ash'arite *kalam* to be the principal representative of scholastic fideism in Islam. Since al-Ash'ari holds that revelation precedes reason in determining the truth of religious belief, he is an adherent of anti-rationalistic fideism. Unlike the traditionalist fideists, such as the Hanabilah, however, he has no problem in employing *kalam* to defend religious doctrine. He is therefore a scholastic fideist. Although the rise of scholastic fideism is closely associated with al-Ash'ari, its roots go back to the Mu'tazilites, as explained earlier. Although the Mu'tazilites were certainly not fideists, they did provide a major contribution to the synthesis of al-Ash'ari's new theology by being pioneers of *kalam*. As A. J. Wensinck puts it, "al-Ash'arī ... was destined to deal the death-blow to Mu'tazilism, not, however, without being infected by its essence."[44]

Later, famous scholastic fideists who were Ash'arites include Abu Bakr al-Baqillani (d. 1013), al-Baghdadi (d. 1037), al-Juwayni (d. 1085)[45] and al-Juwayni's most famous student and arguably the greatest Ash'arite thinker produced by Islam, Abu Hamid al-Ghazali (d. 1111).[46] In the works of these thinkers, the Ash'arite theological and methodological framework is clearly in operation. For instance, in al-Baqillani's *The Book of the Introduction (Kitab at-tamhid)*, traditionalist Islamic doctrine is explicated and defended through *kalam* style argumentation.[47] Something similar can be seen in al-Juwayni's *The Guide to the Cogent Proofs of the Principles of Faith (Kitab al-irshad ila qawati 'al-adilla fi usul al-I'tiqad)*.[48] And in al-Ghazali's *magnum opus, The Incoherence of the Philosophers (Tahafut al-falasifa)*,[49] one finally sees the eclipse of theistic rationalism in Islam by anti-rationalistic fideism defended by Ash'arite *kalam*. In one of his later works, al-Ghazali defines *kalam* as

> the science ... intended to repel errors and heresies [with regard to Islamic beliefs] and to remove doubts [related to them]. Theologians are responsible for this science ... This science is meant to guard the layman's religious belief against the confusion created by heretics.[50]

And with this apologetic understanding of *kalam*, he identifies his approach taken in the *Incoherence*: "With this kind of science [is] related ... the book we composed on the incoherence of the philosophers."[51]

10 *Can Islam be investigated?*

Al-Ghazali's severe criticisms of Islamic philosophy as exemplified by al-Farabi (d. 951) and Ibn Sina (d. 1037) are seen by many as marking the beginning of decline in philosophical output in the Islamic world. Despite the famous response to al-Ghazali by the Spanish Muslim philosopher Ibn Rushd (d. 1198) in his *Incoherence of the Incoherence (Tahafut al-Tahafut)*,[52] the damage done by the former was irreversible. Although perhaps slightly hyperbolic, Akhtar's summary account of al-Ghazali's impact on philosophy seems apt:

> The battle for philosophy, which began with Al-Kindī, was won for religion by Al-Ghazālī who was distressed by the impiety of excessive confidence in the prowess of philosophical reason at the expense of revealed guidance and by the heretical conclusions that reason sometimes reached. Islamo-Hellenistic philosophy formally ended with Ibn Rushd; it was suffocated by the forces of orthodoxy ... Ever since his single-handed demolition of the Islamic philosophical edifice, ordinary Muslims have concurred with Al-Ghazālī that philosophy fathers unnecessary doubts and hesitations, raises questions about the duties of faith and replaces revealed certainties with the ambiguities, confusions and conjectures of unaided reason.[53]

The perceived triumph of anti-rationalistic fideism over theistic rationalism in Islam has, after al-Ghazali, remained a popular view; indeed, after his attack on philosophy, anti-rationalistic fideism continues to dominate discussions about the truth of religious matters.

3. Responding to anti-rationalistic fideism as an important preliminary to a philosophical investigation of Islam

A philosophical investigation of Islam gives priority to reason over revelation in determining the truth of Islamic belief. As should be clear by now, however, prioritizing reason in this way will be rejected by those Muslims who are anti-rationalistic fideists, of both the traditionalist and scholastic kind. Given the current prevalence of anti-rationalistic fideism in Islam, such a rejection should not be taken lightly, especially if philosophical investigations of the Islamic faith are to be taken seriously by Muslims. Over the course of Chapters 2–4, I will offer an assessment of Islamic anti-rationalistic fideism, dividing it into an examination of 'classical' and 'contemporary' accounts. In critically assessing classical traditionalist fideism in Islam, I will focus on a prominent thinker from the Hanabilah. My assessment of classical scholastic fideism in Islam will be done by looking at a prominent historical figure from the Ash'arite tradition. Following this, I will evaluate the merits of some anti-rationalistic fideistic arguments as found in the works of some contemporary Muslim thinkers. All of this I see as an important clearing of the ground before presenting my philosophical assessment of the Muslim faith.

Can Islam be investigated? 11

Notes

1 Ibn Khaldun, *The Muqaddimah*, trans. by Franz Rosenthal, Vol. 3, Second Edition, (Princeton: Princeton University Press, 1958), p. 250.
2 Ibid., pp. 252–253.
3 Shabbir Akhtar, *A Faith for All Seasons*, (Chicago: Ivan R. Dee, 1990). p. 34. Although I agree with Akhtar's general point about the dominance of fideism among Muslim thinkers today, I think that his definition of 'fideism' is too simplistic and does not take into consideration the various ways in which it can be understood in Islamic thought. As I explain later in this chapter (and as will become clear in subsequent chapters), there are several different interpretations of what, precisely, fideism amounts to in Islam.
4 Binyamin Abrahamov, *Islamic Theology: Traditionalism and Rationalism*, (Edinburgh: Edinburgh University Press, 1998), pp. ix–x.
5 Ibid., p. ix.
6 Ibn Hanbal, 'Tabaqāt al-Hanābilah', in Kenneth Cragg and R. Marston Speight (eds.), *Islam from Within: Anthology of a Religion*, (Belmont: Wadsworth Publishing Company, 1980), p. 126. Scholars disagree whether Ibn Hanbal is actually the author of the creedal statement found in this text. Still, as Cragg and Speight write: "[Although] [i]t is difficult to say definitely whether Ibn Hanbal actually composed this text, ... there is no reason to consider its content as other than an authentic expression of his ideas" (ibid, p. 118).
7 Wesley Williams, 'Aspects of the Creed of Imam Ahmad Ibn Hanbal: A Study of Anthropomorphism in Early Islamic Discourse', *International Journal of Middle Eastern Studies*, 34, (2002), p. 442.
8 George Makdisi, 'Hanabilah', in Mircea Eliade (ed.), *Encyclopedia of Religion*, (New York: Macmillan Publishing Company, 1987), p. 184.
9 This work has been edited and translated into English by George Makdisi. See his *Ibn Qudama's Censure of Speculative Theology*, (Cambridge: Gibb Memorial Trust, 1962).
10 Wael B. Hallaq has an excellent translation of this work. See his *Ibn Taymiyya Against the Greek Logicians*, (Oxford: Clarendon Press, 1993).
11 See Fazlur Rahman, *Islam*, (Chicago: University of Chicago Press, 1979), pp. 87–88. Other scholars entertain different historical accounts of the origin of the name 'Mu'tazilites'. See D. Gimaret's article 'Mu'tazila in *Encyclopaedia of Islam*, ed. C. E. Bosworth et al., (Leiden: E.J. Brill, 1993), Vol. 7, p. 783ff.
12 Gimaret, 'Mu'tazila', p. 791.
13 Ibid., pp. 791–792.
14 'Abd al-Jabbar, *Kitab al-Usul al-khamsa*, trans. Richard C. Martin et al., *Defenders of Reason in Islam*, (Oneworld, 1997), p. 90. The 'five fundamentals' referred to in the title of this work are five tenets, belief in which made one a person who subscribed to the Mu'tazilite theological outlook. 'Abd al-Jabbar states them as follows in his work:

> There are five fundamentals of religion: [Divine] unicity (*tawhid*), [Divine] justice (*'adl*), the promise and the threat [made by God] (*al-wa'd wa l-wa'id*); the intermediate position [regarding the fate of grave sinners] (*al-manzila bayn al-manzilatayn*); and commanding the good and prohibiting evil (*al-amr bi l-ma'ruf wa l-nahy 'an l-munkar*).
>
> (Ibid, p. 91)

Prior to belief in any of these tenets, however, is the knowledge of God that one acquires using one's reason, according to 'Abd al-Jabbar and other Mu'tazilites.
15 Rahman, *Islam*, p. 88.

12 Can Islam be investigated?

16 For an excellent introduction to and survey of *'Ilm al-kalām*, see L. Gardet's entry on "Ilm al-kalām' in the *Encyclopaedia of Islam*, ed. Bernard Lewis et al., (Leiden: E.J. Brill, 1971), Vol. 3, pp. 1141ff.

17 Majid Fakry, *A History of Islamic Philosophy*, Third Edition, (New York: Columbia University Press, 2004), p. 64.

18 Ibid.

19 Ibid.

20 W. Montgomery Watt, *Islamic Philosophy and Theology: An Extended Survey*, Second Edition, (Edinburgh: Edinburgh University Press, 1985), p. 65.

21 Ibid., p. 64.

22 Ibid., p. 65.

23 Ibid. For another detailed account of al-Ash'arī's conversion, see the introduction by Walter C. Klein in his translation of Al-Ash'arī's *Al-Ibānah 'An Usūl Ad-Diyānah* (The Elucidation of Islam's Foundations), (New Haven: American Oriental Society, 1940), pp. 27–28.

24 Klein, *Al-Ibānah*, p. 27.

25 Literally, the word means the 'trodden path'; in an Islamic context, however, it refers to 'the way of the Prophet'. Typically, reference to the Sunnah is made by citing *hadiths* (reports of prophetic tradition) that contain sayings and actions attributed to the Prophet Muhammad.

26 Ibid., pp. 27–28.

27 Watt, *Islamic Philosophy and Theology*, p. 65.

28 Ibid.

29 Klein, *Al-Ibānah*, p. 46.

30 Ibid., p. 49.

31 Ibid., pp. 49–50.

32 Watt, *Islamic Philosophy and Theology*, p. 66.

33 This work has been translated into English by Richard J. McCarthy. See his *The Theology of Al-Ash'arī*, (Beyrouth: Imprimerie Catholique, 1953).

34 Ibid., p. 5. What is salient in this description is that al-Ash'arī is not merely *stating* a creed in this work, but, as he says, also providing *arguments* in defense of traditionalist Islamic doctrine.

35 Ibid., p. 6.

36 See Qur'an 22:5 and 23:14. 22:5 is often cited by Muslim thinkers as proof for the resurrection, and *a fortiori*, the existence of God.

37 Ibid, pp. 6–7.

38 Ibid., p. 7.

39 Arent J. Wensinck, *The Muslim Creed*, (London: Frank Cass & Co., 1965), p. 68.

40 Klein, *Al-Ibānah*, p. 31. In opposing attempts to rationally question the truth of Islamic doctrine, Al-Ash'ari is, like the Hanabilah, an anti-rationalistic fideist. But his fideism is of a more sophisticated form. As Majid Fakhry writes,

> If [Al-Ash'ari's] theological position, expressed in the classical formula *bilā kayfa* (ask not how) must be described as agnostic, it is nonetheless to be clearly distinguished from the blind agnosticism of the religious bigot who will entertain no questions whatsoever. For his was the qualified agnosticism of the earnest seeker who ends up by asserting, rightly or wrongly, the inability of reason to plumb the mystery of man in relation to God, or of God to man.
>
> *A History of Islamic Philosophy*, Third Edition, (New York: Columbia University Press, 2004), p. 215.

41 Khaldun, *Muqaddimah*, p. 34.

42 Ibid., pp. 49–51.

Can Islam be investigated? 13

43 Francis E. Peters, *A Reader on Classical Islam*, (Princeton: Princeton University Press, 1994), p. 358.
44 Wensinck, *The Muslim Creed*, p. 87.
45 For a discussion of these thinkers and others who belonged to the Ash'arite school, see Watt, *Islamic Philosophy and Theology*, Chapter 12.
46 See ibid., Chapter 13.
47 Ibid., pp. 76–77.
48 For an English translation of this work, see Paul E. Walker and Muhammad S. Eissa, *A Guide to The Conclusive Proofs for The Principles of Belief*, (Reading: Garnet Publishing, 2001).
49 An excellent translation of this work has been done by Michael E. Marmura, (Provo: Brigham Young University Press, 1997).
50 Al-Ghazali, *The Jewels of the Qur'ān*, trans. and ed. by Muhammad Abul Quasem, (Kuala Lumpur: University of Malaysia Press, 1977), p. 38.
51 Ibid.
52 The standard English translation of this work is by Simon van der Bergh, (London: Trustees of the E.J.W. Gibb Memorial, 1978).
53 Shabbir Akhtar, *The Quran and the Secular Mind*, (London and New York: Routledge, 2008), p. 81.

2 Classical traditionalist fideism in Islam

1. Ibn Qudama – a representative of traditionalist fideism in Islam

Traditionalist fideism in Islam as exemplified by the Hanabilah has a strong tendency to reject *any* kind of attempt at philosophical speculation in the domain of religious belief. As we saw in the previous chapter, traditionalist fideists reject theistic rationalism and the application of the philosophical method to Islamic belief. This is not limited to the efforts of the Mu'tazilites and later Islamic philosophers, such as al-Farabi (d. 950) and Ibn Sina (d. 1037), but also includes the more religiously conservative approach of speculative theology (*kalam*) of the sort practiced by al-Ash'ari.

In this chapter, I will consider whether the austere fideism of the traditionalist sort poses any real challenge to the legitimacy of philosophically investigating Islamic belief. In particular, I will assess whether, from a Muslim perspective, traditionalist fideism offers us any good reasons to forego a philosophical investigation of Islam. A good classical representative of the traditionalist fideists in Islam is the Hanbalite theologian Muwaffaq ad-Din b. Qudama (d. 1223), whose work *A Thesis on Prohibiting the Study of Works by the Partisans of Speculative Theology* (*Mas'ala fi tahrim an-nazar fi kutb ahl al-kalam*)[1] is an excellent compendium of typical arguments used by defenders of traditionalist fideism in an Islamic context.[2] The broad aim of Ibn Qudama's 13th-century treatise is to argue that any sort of rational speculation, including speculative theology (*kalam*), is impermissible in discussions about Islamic belief. A careful evaluation of the arguments that Ibn Qudama presents in his treatise will be helpful in considering the plausibility of traditionalist fideism in Islam and what obstacles, if any, it poses to philosophical investigations of Islamic belief.

The immediate context of Ibn Qudama's composition was to warn the people of his town in Damascus against the dangers of speculative theology. In this work, Ibn Qudama concentrates his efforts on responding to the views of another Hanbalite theologian, Ibn 'Aqil (d. 1119), who had for a period heretically expounded the views and endorsed the methods of Mu'tazilite *kalam* – the focal point of Ibn Qudama's attack. For Ibn Qudama, Mu'tazilite *kalam* represented

Classical traditionalist fideism in Islam 15

the origin of the heresies that were propagated by Ibn 'Aqil. As George Makdisi explains, according to Ibn Qudama, it was the Mu'tazilite system of thought that was the "source of pollution" giving rise to various heresies, such as allegorical interpretation of the divine attributes mentioned in the Qur'an (pp. xv–xvi). So, although Ibn Qudama's polemic is targeted at a specific individual, his censure has wider applicability. Makdisi further explains:

> [T]he scope of the treatise transcends the narrow confines of a refutation of one Hanbalite by another; for the brunt of Ibn Qudāma's attack is directed against *all* manner of speculation in matters of religious belief. Such speculation, reiterates Ibn Qudāma, is unorthodox. It is a heretical innovation. All those who indulge in it are to be declared heretical, no matter what their particular school may be ... [B]eyond Ibn 'Aqīl are not only the Mu'tazilites ... but also the Aš'arites, their intellectual heirs, who parade under the guise of orthodoxy. All of these people have one thing in common ... they are partisans of the heretical science of speculative theology.
>
> (p. xvi; italics mine)

Construed more generally, then, Ibn Qudama's treatise provides us with a formulation and defense of a rather strict form of fideism that rejects the use of rational speculation in discussions of religious belief, the sort I have termed traditionalist fideism. Indeed, Makdisi goes as far as describing Ibn Qudama's position on faith and reason as 'Tertullianist' (p. xix), referring to the Church father Tertullian (d. 222) who is well known for his antagonism towards philosophical speculation about religious matters. The similarity between Ibn Qudama and Tertullian, says Makdisi, comes from the fact that "both shared an intense hatred for dialectic and rational speculation in matters of religious belief" (ibid).

Distilled to its essentials, Ibn Qudama's polemic against Ibn 'Aqil supplies two main arguments in favor of traditionalist fideism and against the permissibility of engaging in speculative theology – (1) an Argument from Authority and (2) an Argument against *Ijtihad* (roughly translated as 'independent critical thought') in matters of religious belief.[3] In what follows, I will give an account of these two arguments before turning to a critical examination of them to see whether they have any force in precluding philosophical investigations of Islamic belief.

2. Ibn Qudama's arguments against speculative theology (*kalam*)

2.1 The Argument from Authority

Ibn Qudama's first and main argument against the permissibility of engaging in speculative theology consists of an appeal to the three-tiered authority of

16   *Classical traditionalist fideism in Islam*

the Qur'an, *Sunnah* and scholarly consensus (*'ijma*). The authority of these three sources forbids one from engaging in speculative theology, says Ibn Qudama, before concluding that its practice is therefore impermissible.

(1) The Qur'an: Ibn Qudama does not explicitly discuss whether the Qur'an disapproves of speculative theology. He does, however, give an indirect argument to this effect. In reference to the matter of how one should understand or interpret Qur'anic verses that mention the divine attributes (one of the main areas of interest for practitioners of speculative theology), Ibn Qudama argues that the great Ancestors (*Salaf*)[4] simply accepted such verses with "unreserved approval" (p. 7). They did not interpret these verses allegorically based on some sort of rational argument for the conclusion that a literal interpretation of the divine attributes would be implausible. The argument here appears to be the following. If the Qur'an had permitted speculative theology, the great Ancestors would have engaged in it. But this did not happen:

> It is agreed among traditionists, orthodox and schismatics alike, that the doctrine of the Ancestors as regards the attributes of God, consisted in acknowledging them, allowing them to pass intact, submitting unreservedly to their Author, and avoiding the temerity of undertaking their interpretation.
>
> (Ibid)

Therefore, concludes Ibn Qudama, the Qur'an does not approve of speculative theology.

(2) The *Sunnah*: Ibn Qudama proceeds to argue that a similar point applies to the traditions of the Prophet in which the divine nature is mentioned. These were "pass[ed] intact as they had come down from the Prophet" and thus the traditionalists ('true Muslims', for Ibn Qudama) follow suit by giving "unreserved approval to those traditions treating of the names of God and His attributes" (p. 8). The argument suggested here seems to be this. If speculative theology were permitted, then the great Ancestors (whom Muslims generally regard as the best Muslims to have lived) would have practiced it when considering the content of the Prophetic traditions in which the divine attributes are mentioned. Since they didn't do this, the practice of speculative theology must consequently be impermissible.

(3) Scholarly consensus (*'ijma*): Scholarly consensus also speaks against speculative theology, says Ibn Qudama, since the great Imams condemned it. One of the Imams he cites is al-Shafi'i, who is reported to have said:

> My judgment with respect to the partisans of speculative theology is that they be smitten with fresh leafless palm branches, that they be paraded among the communities and tribes, and that it be proclaimed: "this is the punishment of him who has deserted the Book [i.e., the Qur'an] and the Sunna, and taken up speculative theology."
>
> (p. 12)

Classical traditionalist fideism in Islam 17

Ibn Qudama cites several other Islamic scholars who echoed similar repudiations of speculative theology and goes on to say that "[t]he censure of speculative theology is abundant" (ibid). Moreover, the Imams and learned men, he goes on to argue, urged the Muslim community to follow the example of the great Ancestors who, as already mentioned, did not engage in speculative theology (p. 13).

For Ibn Qudama, the joint authority of the Qur'an, the *Sunnah* and scholarly consensus (*'ijma*) constitutes a decisive condemnation and refutation of the claim that engaging in speculative theology is permissible from an Islamic perspective. His Argument from Authority is succinctly formulaic in the following passage:

> [D]o you suppose that we shall desert the word of God, and the word of His Apostle, and the admonition of our Imāms urging us to follow our Ancestors, in order to accept Ibn 'Aqil's advice when he says: "Leave off following their example! Imitate me, and follow my teachings and the teachings of speculative theologians like me."
>
> (p. 16)

It is clear from an examination of his treatise that Ibn Qudama takes his Argument from Authority to be a sufficient refutation of the claim that engaging in speculative theology is permissible from an Islamic perspective. As he explains, the Qur'an, *Sunnah* and scholarly consensus jointly constitute a "decisive proof" in religious matters (p. 17), and examining them, he says, reveals that the practice of speculative theology is impermissible.

2.2 *The Argument against* Ijtihad

In his treatise, Ibn Qudama offers an argument against the speculative theologians who maintain that people require rational proof by way of *ijtihad* upon which to ground their religious beliefs, as opposed to simply following religious authority (ibid). This argument is broadly structured as follows. The speculative theologian's claim entails that there is "an obligation upon the common people to make use of [*ijtihad*] in the minutiae of daily affairs and religious beliefs," but "this is wrong for several reasons" (ibid). If requiring the common people to take up *ijtihad* is unacceptable, then the speculative theologian's claim is wrong. In support of his view that common people are under no obligation to reflect critically about Islamic beliefs through the process of *ijtihad*, Ibn Qudama presents five separate arguments.

(1) The first argument is this. If the speculative theologian's claim that one is required to examine the rationality of Islamic beliefs through *ijtihad* is correct, this means that the Prophet is guilty of "a fault of omission" (ibid). This is because, according to Ibn Qudama, the Prophet never ordered anyone in his community to assess the reasonableness of Islamic belief using

18 *Classical traditionalist fideism in Islam*

rational proofs and arguments. On the contrary, he was content with simple submission. But then we have a problem for the speculative theologian:

> Do you suppose that the Prophet be wrong in accepting ... simple submission to God, rather than that they [i.e., the people of his community] should learn the science of speculative theology and examine the "accident", the "substance", and the "body;" and, on the other hand, that the speculative theologians be right with respect to the transgression of him who neither learned nor examined those things?
>
> (p. 18)

If the speculative theologian were to answer yes, he or she cannot really be Muslim: "If this be so, then let them claim for themselves a law and a system of worship other than that of Islam, and leave alone Muhammad's religion!" (ibid).

(2) Ibn Qudama's second argument against *ijtihad* cautions against several undesirable consequences that would follow if everyone is required to examine the rationality of their religious convictions through *ijtihad*. A dangerous slippery slope would arise (ibid). The time and effort required to engage in *ijtihad* would mean that people simply would not have time for other important matters: "The world would lie in waste, people would perish, progeny would become extinct, holy war would become neglected, and countries would become ruined" (ibid). But this cannot be, says Ibn Qudama, since God Himself tells us that on no soul does He place a burden greater than it can bear (see Qur'an 2:286).

(3) Ibn Qudama's third argument is very brief. *Ijtihad* cannot be imposed on the common people because, according to scholarly consensus, the masses are not obliged to engage in it. Rather, the masses are perfectly entitled to follow 'the authority of the learned men' in religious matters involving legal prescriptions (ibid). Indeed, there is divine sanction for this view since God Himself orders the common people to ask learned men (see Qur'an 16:43, 21:7) (ibid).

(4) The fourth argument given by Ibn Qudama is comprised of two distinct arguments.

(4.1) Here is the first of the two arguments. Ibn Qudama states that to impose an obligation of *ijtihad* upon everyone "would entail a condemnation of the broad masses to error, by reason of their neglect of that which is incumbent upon them" (ibid). I think that the line of reasoning here is something like this. If *ijtihad* were obligatory upon everyone, then this would mean that the masses are in 'error' by failing to meet certain intellectual obligations (the "neglect of that which is incumbent upon them"). Since most people in the common populace are not practitioners of *ijtihad*, it would follow that such people are failing to meet these intellectual obligations. Ibn Qudama does not elaborate on this argument further, but implicitly suggests that to think the masses are failing in such obligations is somehow unacceptable. Hence, it is wrong to think that the masses are obliged to engage in *ijtihad*.

Classical traditionalist fideism in Islam   19

In further explaining this argument, Ibn Qudama states the following:

> The only thing in respect of which the use of *taqlīd* [roughly translated as 'to follow or imitate someone without seeking independent evidence'] has been said to be unlawful for them [i.e., the masses] is the manifest ordinance, which they know by virtue of its being manifest, without requiring special pains, thought, or examination; namely, the profession of the unity of God, the mission of Muhammad, the knowledge of the five daily prayers, the fasting of Ramadān, and the rest of the pillars whose religious obligation is of common knowledge. These obligations, having become known by way of *iǧma*, require no study or examination. Therefore, with regard to these obligations, it is unlawful for them to make use of *taqlīd*.
>
> (pp. 18–19)

One problem with what Ibn Qudama says in this passage is that it appears to contain an inconsistency. Ibn Qudama claims that it is unlawful for the masses to resort to *taqlid* in acquiring knowledge of essential Islamic doctrine. This is not to say, however, that Islamic doctrine needs to be reasoned out in accordance with the methods of *ijtihad*. Rather, says Ibn Qudama, knowledge of essential Islamic doctrine (the 'manifest ordinance') comes about 'by virtue of its being manifest'. Hence, it appears that Ibn Qudama is saying that we know about the 'manifest ordinance' *because its truth is manifestly evident*. But, in the same passage, he writes that the manifest ordinance "*become[s] known by way of iǧma*" (emphasis mine). This seems to result in an inconsistency because, on the one hand, the claim is that we know about the manifest ordinance by virtue of its being manifest, and, on the other hand, we know about the manifest ordinance by way of – that is, *inferring from* – scholarly consensus regarding its truth. Attempting to solve this problem need not detain us, however, since Ibn Qudama's basic point here is that the masses know the truth of the 'manifest ordinance', however exactly that might be.[5]

Insofar as we are talking about essential of Islamic doctrine, then, *ijtihad* is not required because belief in its truth is manifest for the masses. It is not 'blind belief' formed because of *taqlid*; rather, it is belief that arises because of the evident truth of essential Islamic doctrine. Now, if the proponent of *ijtihad* accepts this point, and, as a result, qualifies his claim by maintaining that the masses are required to engage in *ijtihad* for specific things such as "the minutiae of religious beliefs and the detailed prescriptions of the practices of worship and of contracts of sale," then he would be foolish: "[N]o one but an ignoramus would profess the obligation of the broad masses to make use of [*ijtihad*] with regard to these matters" (p. 19).[6] Putting aside the *ad hominem* here, there are two reasons why, according to Ibn Qudama, requiring the masses to engage in *ijtihad* for the "minutiae of religious beliefs" is wrong. His first point, which we have already seen, is that this would condemn the masses to error, since the masses generally do not engage in *ijtihad* for such matters. His second point brings us to the second of the two arguments that constitute his fourth overall argument against *ijtihad*.

20 *Classical traditionalist fideism in Islam*

(4.2) Closely connected to the preceding argument is an argument given by Ibn Qudama to the effect that religious faith acquired through rational speculation will lead to uncertainty in religious matters and that such uncertainty in heretical. Suppose, he says, that a person rejects the authority of the great Ancestors and the Imams in understanding and interpreting, for instance, the divine attributes:

> … [W]hat then is he to do? Does he have a way to the knowledge of what is sound in these matters through his own personal effort and rational speculation? When will he at last come to a point at which he will be able to distinguish between a sound argument and a faulty one?
>
> (p. 19)

To illustrate the point, Ibn Qudama asks us to consider Ibn 'Aqil, who "exhausted his total capacity on speculative theology, along with all his intelligence and sagacity" but "did not prosper, nor … succeed in the right direction" (p. 19). Engaging in *ijtihad* or speculative theology will surely lead one to heretical innovations and wrongdoing. If someone such as Ibn 'Aqil, who exhausted all his intellectual capacities on speculative theology, did not prosper, then the prospects for the average person in the common populace to succeed in the practice of rational speculation about religious matters will, *a fortiori*, be very dim indeed.

(5) Ibn Qudama's fifth and final argument against *ijtihad* is an indirect argument based on nine cumulative reasons that allegorical interpretation of the divine attributes is forbidden. Since what Ibn Qudama discusses as part of this argument is mostly related to the permissibility of allegorical interpretation, rather than a general discussion of *ijtihad* or speculative theology, I shall forego an analysis of this final argument.

This, then, is my summary account of Ibn Qudama's Argument from Authority and Argument against *Ijtihad*. These two arguments, if successful, serve to support the traditionalist fideist's position and would thereby provide a basis for rejecting a philosophical investigation of Islam. But are these arguments any good? Let's see.

3. Examining Ibn Qudama's arguments against speculative theology (*kalam*)

3.1 Reply to the Argument from Authority

I will begin with a critical evaluation of Ibn Qudama's Argument from Authority, which is not a good argument because of several objections that can be levelled against it. Here are some, in no particular order:

(1) Ibn Qudama's Argument from Authority rests on what he thinks are authoritative injunctions, found in the Qur'an, the *Sunnah* and the

Classical traditionalist fideism in Islam 21

scholarly consensus, that prohibit the practice of speculative theology. But for such an argument to have persuasive force, even if such injunctions do indeed exist, one must already be committed to the view that these sources are authoritative. The problem here, of course, is that whether these sources *are* authoritative is precisely the sort of issue that those interested in speculative theology may be doubtful about and wish to resolve. Consider, for example, the situation of the doubting Muslim theist who wishes to settle for herself the question whether it is indeed rational to believe that there is a God. It won't do to object to such a theist by telling her that the Qur'an prohibits speculative theology. For, the Qur'an is authoritative in this regard only if it is true that God exists (and has revealed His Will and the relevant Authoritative Commandments in the Qur'an). But it is precisely this belief (or set of beliefs) the reflective Muslim wants to assess; hence, the truth of this belief (or set of beliefs) cannot, given the nature of the dialectic involved, simply be taken for granted. Because of this, Ibn Qudama's Argument from Authority will, at best, have very limited application. It can get off the ground only if one has already submitted to the authority of the Qur'an, the *Sunnah* and the scholarly consensus.

Now, a defender of Ibn Qudama's position might object here that, given the limited scope of his Argument from Authority, so much the worse for the person who does not submit to the authority of the Qur'an, the *Sunnah* and the scholarly consensus. Against this objection, there are at least two possible replies.

One response is that such an objection doesn't tell us what, exactly, the problem is with people who do not submit to the authority of the Qur'an, the *Sunnah* and the scholarly consensus. Let me say a little more here by focusing on the Qur'an only (I will comment on Ibn Qudama's appeal to the *Sunnah* and scholarly consensus later on). Suppose that a doubting Muslim finds herself in a situation where she is considering whether her belief in God's existence is rational. Since the rationality of this belief is under deliberation, this implies that belief in the Qur'an as the Authoritative Word of God would also be under deliberation (this point follows as a straightforward corollary). Here, one needs to ask why a cavalier dismissal of such a Muslim theist and her reflective predicament is necessary or warranted. Suppose that the Qur'an does, as a matter of fact, outlaw speculative theology. If this is the case, then this injunction will have normative force for the doubting Muslim only if she has already submitted herself to the authority of the Qur'an. But, because of her doubt, she is not yet able to submit unreservedly to the authority of the Qur'an. The doubting Muslim is therefore likely to have reservations about alleged Qur'anic injunctions that prohibit the practice of speculative theology. So, in response to Ibn Qudama on this matter, one might ask what is particularly objectionable if a doubting Muslim raises questions about the truth of Islamic belief and related religious injunctions.

22   *Classical traditionalist fideism in Islam*

A second response is to point out that having a dismissive attitude towards those who are interested in the truth or rationality of Islamic belief is not something that can easily be justified using the Islamic Scripture. On the contrary, we find, for instance, the Author of the Qur'an urging those who believe in Him to invite others and graciously argue with them so that they may follow His path: "Invite (all) to the Way of thy Lord with wisdom and beautiful preaching; and *argue* with them in ways that are best and most gracious" (Qur'an 16:125; emphasis mine). True, this verse does not explicitly mention speculative theology, but it does seem plausible that rational speculation about the truth of beliefs is one of the 'best' ways to argue a case in favor of accepting them. Indeed, the Qur'an seems open to this point more specifically with respect to religious beliefs. A clear case in point, among several possible examples, is the Qur'anic narrative of Abraham's arguments against his idolatrous community:

> Behold! he [Abraham] said to his father and his people, "What are these images, to which ye are (so assiduously) devoted?" They said, "We found our fathers worshipping them." He said, "Indeed ye have been in manifest error - ye and your fathers." They said, "Have you brought us the Truth, or are you one of those who jest?" He said, "Nay, your Lord is the Lord of the heavens and the earth, He Who created them (from nothing): and I am a witness to this (Truth). And by Allah, I have a plan for your idols - after ye go away and turn your backs." So he broke them to pieces, (all) but the biggest of them, that they might turn (and address themselves) to it. They said, "Who has done this to our gods? He must indeed be some man of impiety!" They said, "We heard a youth talk of them: He is called Abraham." They said, "Then bring him before the eyes of the people, that they may bear witness." They said, "Art thou the one that did this with our gods, O Abraham?" He said: "Nay, this was done by - this is their biggest one! Ask them, if they can speak intelligently!" So they turned to themselves and said, "Surely ye are the ones in the wrong!" Then were they confounded with shame: (they said), "Thou knowest full well that these (idols) do not speak!"
>
> (Qur'an 21:52–65)

In this passage, it is clear that Abraham is resorting to some sort of rational speculation, even if it is rudimentary; he is *reasoning* and *arguing* with the idolaters to show them that they are in 'manifest error'. Notice also that Abraham is *not* satisfied with the idolaters' simple appeal to traditional authority ('we found our fathers worshipping them [the idols]'). One can find other verses in the Qur'an that suggest there is nothing wrong with doubt or self-reflection. Consider once again Abraham who, according to the Qur'an, went through a process of reasoned self-reflection in his search for a being worthy of worship:

> When the night covered him over, He saw a star: He said: "This is my Lord." But when it set, He said: "I love not those that set." When he saw

Classical traditionalist fideism in Islam   23

the moon rising in splendour, he said: "This is my Lord." But when the moon set, He said: "unless my Lord guide me, I shall surely be among those who go astray." When he saw the sun rising in splendour, he said: "This is my Lord; this is the greatest (of all)." But when the sun set, he said: "O my people! I am indeed free from your (guilt) of giving partners to Allah. For me, I have set my face, firmly and truly, towards Him Who created the heavens and the earth, and never shall I give partners to Allah."

(Qur'an 6:76–79)

So, the Qur'an does seem at least open to the possibility that rational speculation is permissible. Given this, one cannot easily dismiss people interested in the rationality of Islamic belief, and the methods of speculative theology, based on a straightforward appeal to the authority of the Qur'an.

(2) One might try to respond to my criticisms given in (1) by arguing that the Qur'an simply *forbids* speculative theology, despite initial appearances to the contrary. Ibn Qudama does provide some indirect considerations in favor of such a conclusion by arguing that *allegorical interpretation of Qur'anic verses that mention the divine attributes* is impermissible. But notice that this claim, even if true, says nothing explicitly about the permissibility of engaging in *speculative theology* in general. In maintaining that one is not permitted to interpret the meaning of the Qur'anic verses that mention various attributes of God, Ibn Qudama is endorsing the well-known principle of *bila kayfa* ('without asking how') in Islamic theology. According to this principle, "one has to accept the sacred text as it is without trying to interpret its modality (*kayfiyya*)."[7] In particular, one must accept apparently anthropomorphic expressions that refer to God without positively ascribing corporeal features to Him.[8] Now, whatever one makes of the plausibility of this principle, it seems to me that its acceptance or denial has no significant bearing on the question whether the practice of speculative theology in general is permissible. For, it seems quite possible to maintain that rational speculation about fundamental Islamic beliefs, such as the existence of God or Muhammad's Prophethood, is permitted, even if inquiring into the modality of the divine attributes is not. A clear example of this position can be found in the works of al-Ash'ari, who, as we have seen, saw no theological objection to constructing rational proofs for the existence of God, even though he explicitly endorsed the principle of *bila kayfa*.

What, then, does the Qur'an say about speculative theology in general? Although the sacred text contains no explicit endorsement or rejection, there are numerous passages in the Qur'an which suggest at the very least that there is nothing wrong or misguided with rational speculation about religious beliefs. I have already mentioned the Qur'anic narratives in which Abraham argues with the idolaters and, on another occasion, reflects

24 *Classical traditionalist fideism in Islam*

rationally about whether certain celestial bodies could ever be contenders for the station of the divine. Apart from such verses, which mention various individuals reasoning with themselves or an audience, there are plenty of other instances where the Qur'an *itself* appears to present arguments *to its readers*. For example, in Surah 52 (*At-Tur*), verses 35–37, we read:

> Were they created by nothing, Or were they themselves the creators, Or did they create the Heavens and the Earth? Nay, but they have no firm belief. Or do they own the treasures of Your Lord? Or have they been given the authority to do as they like?

In a certain *hadith*, a companion of the Prophet, Jubair bin Mu'tim, tells us that he heard him recite these verses once during prayer and that "his heart was about to fly (when [he] realized this firm *argument*)."[9] Indeed, some Muslim thinkers, such as Ibn Rushd, have argued that there are numerous Qur'anic verses which make it abundantly clear that "the [religious] Law urges us to observe creation by means of reason and demands the knowledge thereof through reason."[10] So, despite what Ibn Qudama might have us believe, it is not at all clear that the Qur'an forbids the practice of speculative theology.

(3) If the Qur'an does not forbid speculative theology, what does one say about the great Ancestors who, according to Ibn Qudama, yielded to the authority of the Qur'an but did not engage in speculative theology? If they didn't, doesn't this imply that the practice of the discipline is not permitted for Muslims? I don't think so and here is why. Ibn Qudama argues that the great Ancestors did not interpret the Qur'anic verses in which the attributes of God are mentioned. But, as I have already argued, even if the Ancestors explicitly or implicitly endorsed the principle of *bila kayfa*, this does not mean that they were necessarily opposed to the practice of speculative theology in general. In response to this point, one might argue that the Ancestors also accepted the truth of Islamic doctrine without resorting to rational proofs or arguments. This claim, however, is not obviously true. Even if none of the great Ancestors resorted to detailed rational speculation about the reasonableness of Islamic doctrine, it is hard to believe that *no rational considerations at all* factored into their assessment of the plausibility of Muhammad's claims of being the bearer of God's Final Message to humanity. Still, even if Ibn Qudama is right on this account, there are three further replies one may proffer against his appeal to the authority of the great Ancestors.

(3.1) One response is to point out that the Qur'anic Message, by all traditional accounts, is meant to be *universal*.[11] And if it is universal, then its reasonableness and plausibility is something that all of us will have to consider (or, at least, are permitted to consider). Suppose it is true that some members of the early Muslim community believed in the Qur'anic Message without resorting to any sort of rational speculation about its content. Why should this have a bearing on us now? This point is particularly salient when we see that, in sharp contrast to the religious environment of 7th-century Arabia, we are now living in an age of deep skepticism about the truth and rationality of religious beliefs. Many people will not be content with being told simply to believe without any accompaniment of rational argument.

(3.2) Here is a second response, one that holds even if we regard the opinions of the great Ancestors as authoritative. Suppose that Ibn Qudama is right in maintaining that the Ancestors neither approved of, nor engaged in, speculative theology. One could easily retort that they did not *disapprove* of it or *explicitly censure* its practice. This point seems to me to be true, based on a fair examination of the sources available to us regarding the sayings of the Ancestors. Ibn Qudama does not cite a single example where one of the great Ancestors explicitly repudiated the practice of speculative theology. Hence, it appears arbitrary to interpret their silence on this matter in favor of disapproval rather than approval.[12]

(3.3) A third response to Ibn Qudama's appeal to the authority of the great Ancestors is to ask why their opinions should be regarded as authoritative, or at least why their opinions should be regarded as authoritative *unreservedly*. The great Mu'tazilite theologian, Ibrahim al-Nazzam (d. 840), argued that there are several reasons why one should be cautious about accepting the authority of the great Ancestors.[13] These include inconsistencies in the judgments made by some of the Ancestors, their endorsement of unreliable procedures in accepting traditions attributed to the Prophet, as well as their commitment to many unwarranted assumptions and various biases.[14]

For these reasons, Ibn Qudama's attempt to rule out the permissibility of engaging in speculative theology, based on an appeal to the authority of the Qur'an, fails. All the criticisms I have presented so far can be applied with slight modifications and equal force to Ibn Qudama's attempt to argue, based on the authority of the traditions of the Prophet, that the practice of speculative theology is impermissible.

(4) Having explained some of the problems with Ibn Qudama's appeal to the authority of the Qur'an (problems which also afflict his appeal to the authority of the Prophetic traditions), let me now address his appeal to the *'ijma*, or scholarly consensus. In his attempt to condemn the practice of speculative theology, Ibn Qudama points out that "all of us agree that consensus (*iğmā'*) is a decisive argument" (p. 17). The 'us' here refers to members of the Muslim community. The 'decisive argument' is probably based on a belief held by many Muslims that the truth of a religious matter is infallible when it is agreed upon by scholarly consensus. The basis for this belief appears to be a certain *hadith*, where the Prophet is reported to have said that his community will never agree on an error.[15] If one accepts the authoritative nature of the *'ijma*, then it follows, according to Ibn Qudama, that the practice of speculative theology is forbidden, since there is an infallible consensus that it is.

26   *Classical traditionalist fideism in Islam*

This is not a persuasive argument, even if one accepts the authoritative nature of the *'ijma*. One difficulty here involves what, exactly, the Prophet's referral to his 'community' means. Does the community refer to the Muslim community of *the Prophet's time*, for instance, or *the whole Muslim world*? If we go with the former interpretation, then Ibn Qudama's appeal fails, since there is no explicit disapproval of speculative theology to be found within the Muslim community of the Prophet's time. As we have already seen, one cannot arbitrarily interpret silence in favor of disapproval rather than approval. If, however, we go with the latter interpretation, then Ibn Qudama's appeal to the *'ijma* still fails; there is no consensus among Muslims today that engaging in speculative theology is forbidden. As we saw in the previous chapter, both the Mu'tazilite and Ash'arite schools of thought regarded the practice of speculative theology to be permissible. Now a defender of Ibn Qudama might argue that the *'ijma* is simply defined by the consensus of those who happen to regard speculative theology as impermissible. But this definition is *ad hoc*. To exclude the views and opinions of Muslim thinkers who regard speculative theology as permissible from the rubric of *'ijma* is, without further argument, unjustified. The general problem here is that it is not at all clear how exactly one is to understand and apply the concept of the *ijma*. Unless this difficulty is dealt with, one cannot justifiably appeal to the *'ijma* as supporting the claim that engaging in speculative theology is impermissible.[16]

Because of these objections that can be raised against it, I conclude that Ibn Qudama's Argument from Authority against the permissibility of engaging in speculative theology fails.

3.2 *Reply to the Argument against* Ijtihad

Upon critical examination, Ibn Qudama's Argument against *Ijtihad* fares no better than his Argument from Authority. We have already seen that the latter argument can be rejected for several reasons; hence, one cannot resort to this particular argument to criticize the permissibility of engaging in *ijtihad*.

What about his independent argument against *ijtihad*? The main structure of this argument is a *reductio ad absurdum*; it involves pointing out that the defender of speculative theology, who advocates the practice of *ijtihad*, is committed to a position that says the common populace is obliged to engage in rational speculation about religious belief. Given the (supposed) absurd implications that arise from this supposition, it follows that the common populace has no obligation to engage in such speculation. But this is not a good argument.

Let's begin with the entailment claim. Does the permissibility of engaging in *ijtihad* entail that the common populace is obliged to engage in *ijtihad* and is therefore obliged to engage in rational speculation? I don't think so. A defender of the view that *ijtihad*, or some sort of rational speculation, is permissible in religious matters is not necessarily committed to

Classical traditionalist fideism in Islam   27

the view that it is *obligatory* for *everyone* to think rationally about their religious beliefs. Rather, a more modest proposal could be that it is *permissible* for a *certain* group of people under *certain* circumstances (e.g., when certain theists come to doubt the truth of some of the religious beliefs that they hold). Consider an analogy with a secular discipline such as physics. In saying that rational inquiry about the truth of beliefs about physics is permissible, one need not make the extravagant claim that everyone who has an interest in these beliefs has an obligation to seek out proofs and arguments. Most people in the common populace are content in believing the claims of the relevant expert authorities (i.e., qualified physicists) about these matters. When there is reason for doubt, however, nonexperts may seek rational justification for a certain belief that may be in question. For instance, a nonexpert may have reason to doubt whether a statement made by someone regarding Quantum Theory is true. If so, she may wish to seek rational justification in favor of or against believing in the claim that has been made. But in saying that such a person is permitted to seek rational justification for this belief, one need not also commit oneself to the bolder claim that there is an obligation for all people who hold beliefs about physics to acquire proofs and arguments supporting these beliefs. A similar sort of thing may be said about those thinkers who maintain that engaging in *ijtihad* or rational speculation in religious matters is permissible, given a charitable interpretation of their claims. They are not necessarily committed to the view that rational speculation is obligatory for all individuals who hold religious beliefs. Therefore, Ibn Qudama is wrong; the *permissibility* of engaging in *ijtihad* does *not* entail that *the common populace* is *obliged* to engage in it. Since the entailment claim is false, Ibn Qudama's attempted *reductio* fails and, therefore, so does his Argument against *Ijtihad*.

But suppose we accept, for the sake of argument, that the defender of *ijtihad* or rational speculation in matters about religious belief *does* commit herself to the view that speculation of this kind is required by members of the common populace (excluding obvious cases where this simply cannot apply, for example, in the cases of very young children or the mentally disabled). What is wrong with this view? As we have seen, Ibn Qudama presents five arguments against this position, of which four are relevant. Let's see whether any of these arguments succeed.

(1) The first argument given by Ibn Qudama rests on an appeal to the authority of the Prophet. The Prophet never ordered anyone in his community to engage in speculative theology; he was satisfied with people simply accepting Islamic beliefs based on authority. To demand that people rationally examine their Islamic beliefs is therefore to fault the Prophet for not mentioning the importance of speculative theology. There are several reasons why this argument is a bad one.

(1.1) First, this argument rests on an appeal to authority, an authority that will not be categorically accepted by individuals whose situation

28 *Classical traditionalist fideism in Islam*

involves rational reflection about whether the authority in question is reliable. The force of this argument (even if it is successful), then, will be restricted to people who are already committed to the authority of the Prophet. In my earlier examination of Ibn Qudama's Argument from Authority, I have explained how this limitation affects the worth of this sort of argument.

(1.2) Second, even if one categorically accepts the authority of the Prophet, Ibn Qudama's conclusion does not follow. Supposing it true that the Prophet was silent on whether engaging in rational speculation is permissible, it does not follow that his *silence* is to be interpreted as *disapproval*. Such an inference, as explained earlier, is questionable.

(1.3) A third response is to point out that the Prophet was silent on many disciplines other than speculative theology, which surfaced later. But most Muslims would not regard the practice of these other disciplines as impermissible or maintain that the Prophet was guilty of a fault of omission. This sort of reply is given by Ibn Rushd:

> One cannot maintain that [philosophical] reasoning is an innovation in religion because it did not exist in the early days of Islam. For legal reasoning and its kinds are things which were invented also in later ages, and no one thinks they are innovations. Such should also be our attitude towards philosophical reasoning.[17]

Although a defender of Ibn Qudama could conceivably argue in response that legal reasoning and other such disciplines should therefore be jettisoned as well, such a radical move has not to the best of my knowledge been made in the history of Islamic thought. Given this third response, the onus rests with a defender of Ibn Qudama's position to explain why our attitude towards philosophical reasoning should be significantly different from other (permitted) disciplines that emerged after the time of the Prophet.

(1.4) One can add a fourth reply as well. It might be true that the Prophet was satisfied with certain people simply accepting Islamic beliefs based on authority in a historical context where the truth of these beliefs was not really open to reasonable doubt. Commenting on how the people in the Bible knew God, John Hick writes:

> God was known to them as a dynamic will interacting with their own wills, a sheer given reality ... as inescapably to be reckoned with as a destructive storm and life-giving sunshine. ... They did not think of God as an inferred entity, but as an experienced reality. ... To them God was not ... an idea adopted by the mind, but the experiential reality which gave significance to their lives.[18]

Arguably, this is how many characters mentioned in the Qur'an seem to have known God (there is much that is shared between biblical and Qur'anic narratives). It is not implausible to suggest that, for those people living in the religious environment in which the Qur'an was received as a fresh Revelation from God, the Prophet was content with simple acceptance of religious beliefs. This is because as with many of the characters mentioned in the Qur'an, it was obvious to virtually all during the Prophet's time that, for instance, there is a God. Our present situation, however, is significantly different when it comes to the acceptance of religious beliefs. The Prophet was preaching in 7th-century Arabia; we live in the 21st century, after the Copernican Revolution, and after thinkers such as Hume, Kant, Feuerbach and Darwin have given powerful reasons to be skeptical of religious claims. Because of the prevalence of skepticism about the rationality of religious beliefs, it is understandable why many people would be interested in rational speculation about them. But such interest need not come with a charge that the Prophet was culpable for not paying much attention to rational speculation about religious beliefs during his time, since there is a large difference between how religious beliefs were viewed back then and how they are viewed now.

(1.5) A fifth reply that one can give is to question Ibn Qudama's assumption that the Prophet was always silent about rational speculation or content with simple acceptance regarding religious matters. That this was the case in some situations is clear, as one can gather from reading the biography of the Prophet (e.g., the conversion to Islam by Abu Bakr [d. 634], generally regarded by Muslims as the Prophet's closest companion).[19] But in other cases, it does seem that the Prophet wanted his audience to think carefully and rationally about religious beliefs. Consider, as one example, his debate with the Christian chiefs of the delegation of Najran in Saudi Arabia. When the Prophet preached the Islamic message to them, they rejected it. In response, he argued as follows:

'What prevents you from becoming Muslims is your claim that God had a son and your worship of the cross and eating the flesh of swine.' They asked, 'If Jesus was not the son of God, whose son is he then?' and they all argued with him about Jesus. He said, 'Don't you know that there is no son who does not resemble his father?' They agreed. He asked them, 'Don't you know that our Lord is living and does not die, while Jesus' life has come to an end?' They said, 'Yes.' He said, 'Don't you know that our Lord is guardian over everything and protects and sustains living things?' They said, 'Yes.' 'Does Jesus have power over any of this?' They said, 'No.' He said, 'Our Lord has formed Jesus in the womb as He wished, and our Lord does not eat, drink, or excrete.' They said 'Yes.' He said, 'Don't you know that Jesus was borne by his mother as a woman bears a child, and she gave birth to him as any woman gives birth to a child. He was fed like a child and he used to feed, drink and excrete?' They said 'Yes.' So he said, 'How could he then be as you claim?' to which they could not give an answer.[20]

30   *Classical traditionalist fideism in Islam*

Putting aside concerns about the goodness of the argument given by the Prophet, the noteworthy point here is this. If the Prophet did indeed want some people to think carefully and rationally about the Islamic message, as seems to be the case in this exchange he had with a group of Christians, then Ibn Qudama is incorrect; he is wrong in maintaining that the Prophet had always remained silent about rational speculation and did not intellectually engage with his audience about religious matters.

(2) Let's now consider Ibn Qudama's second argument against the claim that *ijtihad* is required in matters of religious belief, even for members of the common populace. In this argument, Ibn Qudama appeals to Divine Mercy in an attempt to show that the common people are not required to engage in rational speculation about religious matters. His argument can be summarized as follows:

> P1. An all-merciful God would not put a burden on individuals greater than they can bear.
> P2. Rational speculation in religious matters for individuals of the common populace puts a burden on them greater than they can bear.
>   Therefore,
> C. An all-merciful God would not require rational speculation in religious matters from individuals of the common populace.

This argument fails because the second premise is clearly contestable if not simply false. As explained earlier, the claim that people (including those who belong to the common populace) should engage in rational speculation about religious matters must be understood charitably. One charitable interpretation would be something like this. *Given suitable circumstances* (relating to time, resources, etc.), individuals in the common populace should rationally reflect about the religious beliefs they hold. To make this sort of claim is not to say that we should all become full-time philosophers of religion or that all other important concerns need to be abandoned.

Ibn Qudama argues that an all-merciful God would not overburden his creatures. Suppose we grant this (it seems like a plausible claim to me). The question now is whether engaging in rational speculation about religious matters is too burdensome. Well, it might be if one was required to invest all of one's time and energy into rational investigations of religious claims. But this is not what defenders of rational speculation in religious matters typically maintain. Ibn Qudama's line of reasoning in support of the second premise of this argument consists of a fallacious slippery slope argument. His claim is that if people were to take the initial step of engaging in rational speculation about religious matters, then that would lead to terribly burdensome and disastrous situations. Since no one would want this to occur, people should not take the initial step. But this argument is fallacious because we have no reason to think that engaging in rational speculation about religious matters will lead to burdensome and disastrous

Classical traditionalist fideism in Islam   31

situations. Because a critical premise in Ibn Qudama's argument can be reasonably rejected, his second argument against *ijtihad* fails.

(3) Ibn Qudama's third argument against imposing *ijtihad* on the masses appeals to the scholarly consensus or *'ijma*. Since I have already explained why such an appeal is problematic in arguing that engaging in speculative theology is impermissible, there is no need to address this particular argument again.

(4) Ibn Qudama's fourth argument against requiring the masses to engage in *ijtihad* is, recall, comprised of two distinct arguments, neither of which is successful.

(4.1) One worry that motivates the first argument is that requiring the masses to engage in *ijtihad* would condemn them to the 'error' of neglecting "that which is incumbent upon them." If the masses are required to engage in *ijtihad*, then it follows that they are failing to meet important intellectual obligations, says Ibn Qudama, since it is evident that most people in the common populace do not engage in it. Since such a charge is unacceptable, according to him, it follows that requiring the masses to engage in *ijtihad* is wrong. One problem here is that Ibn Qudama does not explain what is wrong with charging the masses with the failure to meet important intellectual obligations. If his worry is that these obligations would be too burdensome and hard to meet, then the replies I have given to his second argument against *ijtihad* can be used here. Unless some good reasons can be given for thinking that charging the masses with failure to meet certain intellectual obligations is unacceptable, we have no reason to think that leveling such a charge is wrong. Indeed, there are several paradigmatic examples where we *do* clearly maintain that the masses have failed in important intellectual obligations, such as the case of the general German population that regarded the persecution of the Jews by the Nazi regime as acceptable.[21]

(4.2) Another problem with the first of Ibn Qudama's two arguments that collectively constitute his fourth argument against *ijtihad* lies in his claim that the truth of basic Islamic doctrine ('the manifest ordinance') is evident for the masses and that there is therefore no need for rational speculation about religious matters. But this claim is clearly false. What we regard as 'the masses' today is constituted by several different religious and nonreligious groups, many of who do not believe in the truth of Islamic doctrine, much less regard its truth as manifestly evident. Even if we restrict ourselves to the Muslim community, there are several people within this community for whom the truth of Islamic theism is not simply evident. On the contrary, the situation is that it *is* manifestly evident that the truth of Islamic doctrine is *not* manifestly evident! For this reason, several thinkers have argued that one needs to resort to rational speculation to find out where the truth lies in religious matters. As 'Abd al-Jabbar wrote nearly a millennium ago:

[The learned man must speculate in order to obtain knowledge of God] because if he hears the people's controversies concerning these systems

32 *Classical traditionalist fideism in Islam*

of thought, the charge of unbelief through which they accuse each other (*takfīr*) and each of them frightening his colleague as a result of the controversy, and if he knows that it is impossible that all these systems of thought should be right, for each contradicts the other, for example the notion that the world is eternal vis-à-vis the notion that the world was created, the notion that God can be seen vis-à-vis the notion that He cannot be seen, and [if he knows] that it is also impossible that all these systems can be wrong, for the truth lies within one of them, that is, it is inconceivable that the world should not be eternal and should not have been created, [he will necessarily know that] there are systems which are right and others which are wrong.[22]

(**4.3**) The gist of Ibn Qudama's other argument is that rational speculation in the domain of religious belief will lead to uncertainty about religious matters and that this is unacceptable. Such speculation is therefore not permissible. This argument is not a good one. Against it, two replies may be given. First, it is questionable whether engaging in rational speculation will necessarily lead to uncertainty about religious matters (or greater uncertainty) than not engaging in any rational speculation whatsoever. This latter point is an important one. Typically, those who are interested in rational speculation about religious belief wish to dispel what they perceive to be uncertainties surrounding such belief. It might very well be that, in engaging in rational speculation about religious matters, the situation of uncertainty is *alleviated* even if it is not *eliminated*. Second, one can ask why arriving at uncertain conclusions in religious matters should be regarded as unacceptable. Ibn Qudama simply condemns this point as heretical, but without any supporting evidence. Rather than constituting heresy, it might be that an acknowledgement of uncertainty in religious matters is part of an adequate religious outlook.

None of the four arguments given by Ibn Qudama against *ijtihad* succeed. An overall consideration of his Argument against *Ijtihad* shows that it is no better than his Argument from Authority.

4. Some concluding remarks about classical traditionalist fideism in Islam

In this chapter, I have argued that neither Ibn Qudama's Argument from Authority nor his Argument against *Ijtihad* succeeds. These arguments, as I explained earlier, support a particularly austere form of fideism that I have called traditionalist fideism. Since this sort of fideism maintains that rational speculation about religious matters is not permitted, Ibn Qudama's arguments may also be construed as arguments against any endeavor to philosophically investigate the Islamic faith. Moreover, since he is an excellent representative of the classical traditionalist fideists

Classical traditionalist fideism in Islam 33

in Islam, the failure of Ibn Qudama's arguments carries with it two significant points. First, insofar as he exemplifies the position of the classical traditionalist fideists in Islam, the criticisms of Ibn Qudama that I have presented in this chapter serve to highlight the weaknesses in their position. Second, since the position of the classical traditionalist fideists rejects theistic rationalism, my critical assessment of the former has revealed several unsuccessful ways of repudiating theistic rationalism from a fideistic perspective.

Given the considerations presented in this chapter, it seems to me that the task of philosophically investigating Islam has not been shown to be unacceptable based on the general position adopted by defenders of classical traditionalism fideism in Islam. At this point, those who wish to protest a philosophical investigation of Islam from a Muslim perspective might shift their focus and maintain that such an investigation is nevertheless objectionable, given some of the arguments offered by the scholastic fideists in Islamic thought. Whether Islamic scholastic fideism poses a barrier to a philosophical investigation of Islam is a question I turn to in the next chapter.

Notes

1 In this chapter, I will be referring to the translation of this work by George Makdisi titled *Ibn Qudama's Censure of Speculative Theology*, (Cambridge: E. J. W. Gibb Memorial Trust, 1962). Henceforth, page references in the main text, unless otherwise stated, will be to this work.

2 As James Pavlin notes, in Ibn Qudāma's treatise against *kalām* "we see a fairly well developed summary of the traditionalist opposition to the *mutakallimūn* [scholastic theologians]," 'Sunni Kalām and Theological Controversies', in S. H. Nasr and O. Leaman (eds.), *Routledge History of Islamic Philosophy*, (New York: Routledge, 1996), p. 115.

3 Ibn Qudama's treatise does address other matters. Since, however, these are peripheral to the central arguments and criticisms he offers against *kalam*, they need not concern us for present purposes.

4 This word in Arabic literally means 'ancestors' or 'predecessors'; in Islamic terminology, however, it is generally used to refer to the first three generations of Muslims.

5 Perhaps there is a way to remove the inconsistency here. If by *taqlid* one means *an act of conscious deliberation to submit to religious authority*, then it might be argued that the masses do not engage in it since such conscious deliberation is typically absent in their acquisition of religious beliefs. It might be that Ibn Qudama thinks religious beliefs held by the masses constitute knowledge because their truth is simply evident, and the reason their truth is evident is because of what is proclaimed (correctly as the truth) by way of the *'ijma*. The surrounding religious environment, formed and shaped by what is proclaimed through the *'ijma*, might be such that knowledge of religious truth is evident to all without any act of conscious deliberation being required. And if there is no conscious deliberation on the part of the masses in acquiring religious belief by submitting to religious authority, then it might be argued that they do not acquire such belief based on *taqlid*. Perhaps this sort of move dissolves the charge of inconsistency. I am not sure. All I am suggesting here is a way to nuance the

34 *Classical traditionalist fideism in Islam*

issue for further discussion, which, for our present purposes, need not involve us any further.

6 Makdisi's English translation contains a crucial error here, which I have corrected in this quote. In the original text, the word *taqlid* appears when it should be *ijtihad*.

7 Binyamin Abrahamov, 'The Bi-lā Doctrine and its Foundations in Islamic Theology', *Arabica*, tome XLII, (Leiden: E.J. Brill, 1995), p. 365. Abrahamov's paper provides a useful survey of the doctrine of *bila kayfa* in Islamic theology.

8 Ibid., pp. 365–366.

9 Sahih al-Bukhari, Volume 6, Book 60, Number 377, available online at https://muflihun.com/bukhari/60/377.

10 Ibn Rushd, *On the Harmony of Religions and Philosophy* (*Kitab fasl al-maqal*), available online at www.muslimphilosophy.com/ir/art/irl00.htm.

11 Traditional Muslims who make this point typically draw our attention to the fact that the Qur'an addresses a wide range of people and sometimes addresses humankind in general. It also says that the Prophet, the bearer of God's Final Message, was sent as a mercy for *all* creatures (Qur'an 21:107).

12 This argument is presented in a treatise attributed to al-Ash'ari titled *Risāla (Fī) Istihsān Al-Khawd Fī 'Ilm Al-Kalām* ('A Vindication of The Science of Kalam'), edited and translated into English by Richard McCarthy in *The Theology of Ash'arī*, (Beirut: Imprimerie Catholique, 1953). See esp. pp. 121–122.

13 Abrahamov, *Islamic Theology: Traditionalism and Rationalism*, pp. 46–47.

14 Ibid.

15 At-Tirmidhi, Book 31, Hadith 2167, https://muflihun.com/tirmidhi/31/2167.

16 For a good discussion of this problem, see Wael Hallaq, 'On The Authoritativeness of Sunni Consensus', *International Journal of Middle Eastern Studies*, 18, (1986), pp. 427–454.

17 Rushd, *On the Harmony of Religions and Philosophy*, op. cit.

18 John Hick (ed.), *The Existence of God*, (New York: Macmillan Co., 1964), pp. 13–14.

19 See Martin Lings, *Muhammad*, (Unwin Paperbacks, 1988), p. 46ff. As Lings writes, "some of the earliest responses [to the Prophet's claims about receiving Revelations from God] were promoted initially by motives which could not be ascribed to any human attempt to persuade," p. 47.

20 As cited by M. Abdel Hameel, 'Early kalām', in Oliver Leaman and Seyyed Hossein Nasr (eds.), *History of Islamic Philosophy*, (New York: Routledge, 2001), pp. 77–78.

21 This is, of course, an extreme case, but it serves to enforce the point being made here. Consider also several more mundane cases, where lots of people believe that the Atkins diet is good for you, or that women are the inferior sex, or that racial segregation is morally justified, etc.

22 As quoted by Abrahamov, *Islamic Theology*, p. 59.

3 Classical scholastic fideism in Islam

1. Al-Ghazali – a representative of scholastic fideism in Islam

Scholastic fideism, as we saw in Chapter 2, shares some common ground with traditionalist fideism. While both the scholastic and traditionalist fideists agree that revelation should be the starting point in theological discussions and disputes, scholastic fideism parts from its more stringent cousin in accepting the appropriateness of *kalam*, or scholastic theology. The origin and paradigm example of scholastic fideism in Islam, as explained in Chapter 2, is found in the theological perspective crafted by al-Ash'ari. Perhaps the most historically famous example of a Muslim thinker who subscribed to scholastic fideism is Abu Hamid al-Ghazali, who George Makdisi describes as "the greatest Ash'arite of all."[1] In this chapter, I shall critically examine al-Ghazali's scholastic fideism to see whether it can provide a basis for rejecting philosophical investigations of Islam.

2. Al-Ghazali on the scope and limits of philosophical reasoning about religious matters

No serious discussion regarding philosophical investigations of the Islamic faith would be adequate without considering, at least to some extent, al-Ghazali's criticisms of philosophy. These criticisms were brought out with force in his most famous work on the topic, *The Incoherence of the Philosophers* (*Tahafut al-falasifa*), which, as Michael E. Marmura observes, "marks a turning point in the intellectual and religious history of medieval Islam."[2] Given al-Ghazali's reputation in the Islamic world, his thoughts on religious matters, including Islam's relationship with philosophy, are taken very seriously by Muslims. As W. Montgomery Watt writes, "Al-Ghazālī has sometimes been acclaimed in both East and West as the greatest Muslim after Muhammad, and he is by no means unworthy of that dignity."[3] For his sustained efforts in defending Islamic orthodoxy against systems of thought that were seen as incompatible with Islamic belief, al-Ghazali came to be known within the Muslim tradition as the 'Proof of Islam' (*Hujjat al-Islam*). Part of this defense of Islamic orthodoxy included criticisms of philosophy, and many Muslims today regard al-Ghazali as someone who, in the simple words of Kojiro Nakamura, "refuted philosophy."[4]

36   *Classical scholastic fideism in Islam*

Before I turn to my assessment of al-Ghazali's views on the relationship between Islam and philosophy, it is worth noting that he is by no means an easy figure to understand and interpret. As Richard M. Frank observes in his well-known study:

> Al-Ghazālī shows himself in his writing to be a very complex and problematic personality ... His writings differ greatly from one another in form and rhetoric as well as in topic and focus and in trying to trace the course of his thought and discern his commitments, one has sometimes the impression of attempting to follow the movements of a chameleon, so varied are the hues and postures he assumes from one place to another.[5]

Frank's assessment of al-Ghazali here is not novel. Several centuries earlier, Ibn Rushd famously complained that al-Ghazali "adhered to no one doctrine in his books. Rather, with the Ash'arites he was an Ash'arite, with the Sufis a Sufi, and with the philosophers a philosopher."[6] Because of this problem, my approach to understanding al-Ghazali will be modest. In looking at him as a representative of scholastic fideism, I make no claim whatsoever that my interpretation of al-Ghazali's writings is 'correct'.[7] I do, however, maintain that my analysis of al-Ghazali's writings is based on a plausible interpretation of some of his key ideas, which give rise to some arguments that support the perspective of scholastic fideism.

Although he is difficult to interpret, many scholars nevertheless regard al-Ghazali as a thinker who writes from an Ash'arite perspective or at least as someone who has strong Ash'arite tendencies in him.[8] One thing that clearly situates al-Ghazali within the Ash'arite framework is his position on faith and reason that, in the main, reflects al-Ash'ari's scholastic fideism. The clearest example of al-Ghazali's use of the rational methods of Ash'arite *kalam* in the service of defending Islamic orthodoxy is seen in his *The Incoherence of the Philosophers*.[9] In the 'religious preface' to the *Incoherence*, al-Ghazali makes explicit his motive for writing this work. What troubled him, he writes, was the behavior of a certain group of people who derided Islamic beliefs and rituals:

> I have seen a group who, believing themselves in possession of a distinctiveness from companion and peer by virtue of a superior quick wit and intelligence, have rejected the Islamic duties regarding acts of worship, disdained religious rites pertaining to the offices of prayer and the avoidance of prohibited things, belittled the devotions and ordinances prescribed by the divine law, not halting in the face of prohibitions and restrictions. On the contrary, they have entirely cast off the reins of religion through multifarious beliefs, following therein a troop "who rebel from God's way, intending to make it crooked, who are indeed disbelievers in the hereafter".
>
> (Qur'ān 11:19)[10]

Classical scholastic fideism in Islam   37

This group of freethinkers, al-Ghazali explains, had "no basis for their un-belief other than traditional, conventional imitation [*taqlīd*]."[11] More spe-cifically, their unbelief was based on "hearing high-sounding names such as 'Socrates', 'Hippocrates', 'Plato', 'Aristotle', and their likes"[12] and simply accepting, on the basis of *taqlid*, the erroneous idea (circulated by misguided followers) that these ancient Greek philosophers had repudiated religious law and doctrine.[13] The *taqlid* of the group of freethinkers, says al-Ghazali, is actually *worse* than that of the masses. The reason for this is because the *taqlid* of the masses involves simply accepting the truth (of Islam), whereas that of the freethinkers involves embracing falsehood based on hastiness and the desire to become clever.[14] And so:

> When I perceived this vein of folly throbbing within these dimwits, I took it upon myself to write this book [*The Incoherence of The Philoso-phers*] in refutation of the ancient philosophers, to show the incoherence of their belief and the contradiction of their word in matters relating to metaphysics; to uncover the dangers of their doctrine and its shortcom-ings, which in truth ascertainable are objects of laughter for the rational and a lesson for the intelligent.[15]

Al-Ghazali continues to explain in his religious preface that, contrary to what the group of freethinkers maintain, "all significant thinkers, past and present, agree in believing in God and the last day."[16] Hence, "those prominent and leading philosophers [the freethinker] emulates are inno-cent of the imputation that they deny the religious laws."[17] Nevertheless, the great philosophers are guilty of "straying from the correct path, and leading others astray."[18] Al-Ghazali concludes his religious preface by stating that he will reveal where exactly the philosophers have been de-ceived and have erred.[19]

In the religious preface of the *Incoherence*, al-Ghazali makes it clear that he wants to criticize the philosophers with respect to their deviation from Islamic doctrine. His starting point in discussions of religious matters is, therefore, revelation. Following the religious preface are four separate in-troductions. In the second introduction, al-Ghazali explicitly states that he wishes to take the philosophers to task only for their views that are contrary to religious (Islamic) belief.[20] In the fourth introduction, he reveals that it is in the metaphysical sciences especially where most of the heresies and errors of the philosophers occur.[21] When the philosophers say that logic must be mastered in order to engage in metaphysical speculation, however, they are correct. Al-Ghazali's dispute with the philosophers is not with their endorsement of logic as an instrument nor with their participation in the art of rational speculation; rather, it is with the fact that they have failed to reason properly. In an important and revealing passage of the *Incoherence*, he states that he will

38 *Classical scholastic fideism in Islam*

[follow] their paths expression by expression, and will dispute with them in this book in their language – I mean, their expression in logic. We will make it plain that what they set down as a condition for the truth of the matter of the syllogism in the part on demonstrating [their] logic, and what they set forth as a condition for its form ... [are things] none of which they have been able to fulfil in their metaphysical sciences.[22]

The spirit in which al-Ghazali approaches the philosophers is very much Ash'arite; both he and al-Ash'ari dispute with speculative thinkers, who deviate from Islamic doctrine based on rational arguments, in their own terms. Al-Ghazali does not object to the philosophers, who engage in rational speculation about Islamic belief, in the manner of Ibn Qudama.[23] Instead, his basic argument against them is that none of the unorthodox propositions they entertain have been demonstrated by the standards the philosophers themselves set up. As Marmura notes, the "criterion of demonstrability underlies the whole argument of the [*Incoherence*]."[24] Al-Ghazali finishes the fourth and final introduction to the *Incoherence* by listing twenty such propositions that are contrary to Islamic belief, none of which, as he argues throughout his work, have been demonstrated. His religious motivation for writing the *Incoherence* comes full circle in the conclusion at the end of the work. With respect to three out of the twenty propositions the philosophers and their followers hold as true, they must be condemned as infidels; these are (1) the eternity of the world, (2) God's knowledge of universals but not particulars and (3) denial of bodily resurrection.[25] "These three doctrines," al-Ghazali observes, "do not agree with Islam in any respect."[26] Belief in the other seventeen propositions constitutes heresy but not outright unbelief.[27]

Al-Ghazali's views in the *Incoherence* provide good reason to interpret his overall perspective as Ash'arite. But one can adduce further evidence. The main purpose of the *Incoherence* was to refute, on philosophical grounds, the doctrines of the philosophers that were contrary to Islamic belief. In the *Incoherence*, al-Ghazali tells his readers that, "[a]s regards affirming the true doctrine, we will write concerning it in another book after completing this one."[28] In this promised sequel, titled *Moderation in Belief* (*al-Iqtisad fi al-I'tiqad*), he "expresses his Ash'arite theology in detail."[29] Throughout the pages of the *Incoherence*, al-Ghazali deploys several rational arguments primarily to defend Islamic doctrine. But what value does rational speculation have in positively affirming the truth about Islamic belief?

In *Moderation*, al-Ghazali discloses some important views about the relationship between faith and reason in his discussion of *kalam*. In the exordium to this work, he explains what the correct relationship between the two should be. After praising the adherents of orthodox Islam, he explains that God guided them so that they

came to know the way to reconcile [any] incongruity between the requirements of revelation and the demands of reason. Indeed, they have confirmed that there is no contradiction between the revelation of

Classical scholastic fideism in Islam 39

tradition and the truth of reason. They have come to know that those among the Hashwiyya who believe in the necessity of rigid adherence to imitative belief [*taqlīd*] and the outward form of religion only do so because of [their] poverty of intellect and shortsightedness of vision. And those among the *falāsifah* [philosophers] and the inordinate Mu'tazilites, who commit themselves to the use of reason such that they end up clashing with the definitive pronouncements of revelation, do so out of the wickedness of their minds. Thus, the former group tends toward negligence, the latter toward excess, and both are far from prudence and caution. Indeed, the norm that must be followed in principles of belief is moderation and restraint upon the straight path, and anything that deviates from the proper intent of things is reprehensible.[30]

Here, al-Ghazali condemns, on one hand, an extreme traditionalist group called the Hashwiyya (a group much like, and sometimes identified with, the traditionalist fideists among the Hanabilah) for their uncompromising *taqlid* and abandonment of rational argument, and, on the other hand, the extreme rationalists among the Mu'tazilites and the philosophers for taking reason too far. One group is too negligent and the other is too excessive. The correct path with respect to the principles of Islamic belief is to pursue a course of *moderation*; hence, the title of al-Ghazali's work on Islamic doctrine.

In the rest of the exordium, al-Ghazali comments on the power and limits of reason. Guidance based on reason alone is not possible, unless accompanied by the illuminating "light of revelation."[31] The "capacity of reason is very meager and ... its sphere of action is narrow."[32] Still, reason is like "healthy sight that has no ailment or flaws."[33] But it needs to be complemented by the revelation of the Qur'an, which is like "the sun that shines abroad."[34] Although reason is limited in its capacity, it is nevertheless required to properly understand the revelation of the Qur'an:

> For, someone who declines to use reason, being satisfied with just the light of the Qur'ān, is like someone who stands in the light of the sun with his eyes shut. There is no difference between that person and someone who is blind. For, reason, together with the Qur'ān is "light upon light".
> (Qur'ān 24:35)[35]

Following the exordium in the *Moderation* is a brief explanatory chapter in which al-Ghazali states the main areas of Islamic doctrine that he will elaborate upon and support with rational arguments. There are four main areas which, when taken together, "reduce to the study of God Most High."[36] These pertain to (1) Divine Essence, (2) Divine Attributes, (3) Divine Action, and (4) The Messengers of God.[37] After having explained that rational arguments have a role to play in relation to affirming correct doctrine about these particular religious matters, al-Ghazali presents four short introductory notes; in three of these, he explains the positive function and scope of rational speculation in the realm of Islamic belief.

40   *Classical scholastic fideism in Islam*

In the first of these introductory notes, al-Ghazali argues that rational reflection about religious matters is important. His argument for this is as follows: since various prophets have proclaimed to be bearers of God's Message, people may begin to think that what the prophets say is true after encountering testimony about their doings. Indeed, people should think carefully about what the prophets have said, given the momentousness of the contents of their proclamations. Thus, "the rational man reflects on his destiny."[38]

In the second introduction, al-Ghazali explains that rational reflection is not mandatory for everybody, but only for certain sorts of people. This is because of the specific purpose of rational proofs regarding religious matters. He explains:

> Know that the proofs we will be adducing in this science [of *kalam*] are like medications by which diseases of the heart are treated. If the doctor that uses them is not skillful, having keen intelligence and sound judgment, he might do more harm than good with his medication.[39]

What this passage, and the subsequent discussion in the second introduction of the *Moderation*, reveals is that, for al-Ghazali, one should resort to rational speculation about religious matters only when people deviate from Islamic doctrine, and it should be the last resort. Those people who are simple believers (much like the early community of Muslims), assenting to the truth of Islamic belief without engaging in rational speculation, should be left alone. Introducing such people – 'true believers' as al-Ghazali calls them – to the science of rational speculation regarding religious matters may bring about harmful doubts in their minds.[40] Then there are those who "incline away from the truth, such as the unbeliever and the innovator." Trying to convince these sorts of people with rational proofs is unproductive. Indeed, the "crude and boorish among them … is helped by nothing but the whip and the sword." Most unbelievers and innovators, says al-Ghazali, become more recalcitrant and obstinate whenever one attempts to reason with them about the truth. This does not mean that reason is useless, but simply that the light of reason is a divine gift that God bestows upon a select few. The ignorant, however, "do not comprehend the decisions of reason, just as the light of the sun does not reach the eyes of bats."[41] Another group of people consists of those who believe in religious truth on the basis of authority, but whose faith is shaken either by way of self-reflection or through what they may have heard from others. Such people must be treated with benevolence, and one must do whatever is appropriate to dispel their doubts. This may include simply denouncing the doubts they entertain, reciting from the Qur'an, or relating a Prophetic tradition. Rational proofs should only be the last option, if the person who doubts is "very perceptive and alert [and] who will only be content with reasoned arguments."[42] Finally, there is a group of people who are in error, but in whom one may detect signs of "acumen and perceptiveness." Such people are those who may come to accept the truth. Again, one must treat such people with benevolence and not indulge in "vehement and fanatic

Classical scholastic fideism in Islam 41

argumentation, for that only increases the impulse to go astray and arouses a stubborn obstinacy and willfulness." Instead, one should rely on "gentleness and love" as a guide for bringing to the truth those who are in error.[43]

In the third introduction, al-Ghazali explains that the science of rational speculation is only for those who are qualified to engage in it. In the fourth and final introduction, he discusses the methods of rational proof and argumentation that he will use in the rest of the work. What a careful inspection of these and other parts of the *Moderation* reveals is that, for al-Ghazali, there is an important role for reason in discussions about religious matters, but it is a limited one.

Just how far is philosophical argumentation able to take us, then, in supporting the truth of Islamic belief? In one of his last works, *The Deliverance from Error (al-Munqidh min al-Dalal)*,[44] al-Ghazali explicitly states that both the theologically constrained discipline of *kalam* as well as the religiously neutral science of *falsifah* were unable to satisfy him in his quest for truth about religious matters. Regarding *kalam*, he writes that it was "not sufficient in [his] case" to satiate his quest for religious truth.[45] A similar remark is given regarding *falsifah*: "I knew that philosophy also was inadequate to satisfy my aim fully."[46] But if philosophical considerations cannot show us that Islamic belief is true or may be rationally held, can anything else provide the epistemic foundation for such belief? Al-Ghazali answers this question in the affirmative, claiming that a 'supra-rational' apprehension of religious truths can arise by following the way of the Sufi mystics.[47] In the *Deliverance*, he criticizes both *kalam* and *falsifah*, explaining why neither of them can provide the epistemological foundation for Islamic belief, and presents a defense of what he thinks is a suitable alternative. Al-Ghazali's *Deliverance*, as Watt explains,

> presents us with an intellectual analysis of his spiritual growth, and also offers arguments in defence of the view that there is a form of apprehension higher than rational apprehension, namely, that of the prophet when God reveals truths to him.[48]

In what follows, I shall look at how al-Ghazali's views presented in the *Deliverance* may be taken as posing a challenge to those who are interested in a philosophical investigation of Islam.

3. Al-Ghazali's arguments in *The Deliverance from Error*

3.1 Al-Ghazali's skeptical crisis and fideist resolution

In the introduction to the *Deliverance*,[49] al-Ghazali explains that he is writing in response to his "brother in religion," who requested him to "communicate ... the aim and secrets of the sciences and the dangerous and intricate depths of the different doctrines and views" (p. 61). Since this 'brother' is

42   *Classical scholastic fideism in Islam*

not named in the treatise, it seems plausible to suggest, as McCarthy does, that "the use of the phrase is a literary device ... [and] that [al-Ghazali] is addressing himself to all his Muslim brothers capable of following what he has to say."[50] This is an important hermeneutical point, since it allows us to take al-Ghazali's treatise not just as an autobiographical account of his intellectual journey but also as a summary of his views on religious matters intended for a wider audience.

The first thing that al-Ghazali draws attention to is "the diversity of men in religions and creeds, plus the disagreement of the Community of Islam about doctrines, given the multiplicity of sects and the divergency of methods" (p. 62). He compares this to a "deep sea in which most men founder and from which few only are saved" (ibid). Although salvation will be obtained by only one religious group among the many, each group nevertheless proclaims that *it* will be the one to be saved. This state of affairs, al-Ghazali states, was prophesied in both the Qur'an and in a famous *hadith* of the Prophet (ibid). He explains that, starting from the years of adolescence before he was twenty until the time of writing his treatise when he is over fifty, he constantly plunged into this "profound sea" with "the aim of discriminating between the proponent of truth and the advocate of error, and between the faithful follower of tradition and the heterodox innovator" (ibid).

To grasp "the real meaning of things," writes al-Ghazali, was a disposition that was already in place during his "early years and in the prime of [his] life" (p. 63). Hence, it was only a matter of time before he started reflecting on the problems posed by diversity in beliefs about religion: "I saw that the children of Christians always grew up embracing Christianity, and the children of Jews always grew up adhering to Judaism, and the children of Muslims always grew up following the religion of Islam" (ibid). Since each of these groups have people who hold their respective religious beliefs based on *taqlid* by following their particular teachers, it is necessary to sift through these beliefs in order to discern truth from falsehood (ibid). What follows next is a very important passage in the text worth quoting in its entirety, because, in it, al-Ghazali specifies the type of knowledge he seeks and the criteria for its obtaining:

> So I began by saying to myself: "What I seek is knowledge of the true meaning of things. Of necessity, therefore, I must inquire into just what the true meaning of knowledge is." Then it became clear to me that sure and certain knowledge is that in which the thing known is made so manifest that no doubt clings to it, nor is it accompanied by the possibility of error and deception, nor can the mind even suppose such a possibility. Furthermore, safety from error must accompany the certainty to such a degree that, if someone proposed to show it to be false – for example, a man who [proposed to do so by turning] a stone into gold and a stick into a snake – his feat would not induce any doubt or denial. For if I know that ten is more than three, and then someone were to say: "No,

Classical scholastic fideism in Islam 43

on the contrary, three is more than ten, as is proved by my turning this stick into a snake" – and if he were to do just that and I were to see him do it, I would not doubt my knowledge because of his feat. The only effect it would have on me would be to make me wonder how he could do such a thing. But there would be no doubt at all about what I knew!

(pp. 63–64)

Here, al-Ghazali states that his inquisitive and reflective nature ultimately resulted in a desire to possess "sure and certain knowledge," and he explains the conditions for such knowledge to come about. A careful study of this passage reveals that al-Ghazali specifies four conditions that must jointly obtain for a person to be a possessor of 'sure and certain knowledge'. Schematically, we can represent his criteria as follows:

S has 'sure and certain knowledge' that p if and only if:

1 p is manifestly true to S such that S has no doubt about p.
2 There is no possibility that S is in error or is deceived about it being the case that p.
3 It is inconceivable for S that S is in error or deception about p.
4 S has no doubt about p's indefeasibility.[51]

Conditions (1), (3) and (4) are all 'internal' to the agent. For S to have sure and certain knowledge that p, p must appear to be manifestly true for S to such a degree that there is no doubt in S's mind about p. Moreover, it must be inconceivable for S that she is wrong about p. And, finally, there must be no doubt in S's mind about p's indefeasibility. But all these conditions are related to how the truth about p must appear *to the agent who thinks about p*. It is quite possible for S to be in such a state of mind about p and yet be quite mistaken about p because the 'external' truth about p does not match up with how S views p 'internally' (in her mind). Essentially, the point here is that people can be absolutely convinced (subjectively) that they know p when, in fact, they are externally or objectively wrong. To safeguard against this possibility, al-Ghazali adds 'external' condition (2) so that S's 'cognitive certainties' about p must 'match up' with the way things really are (mind independently) to a degree where there is no objective possibility of error. Only then can the subject be said to possess 'sure and certain knowledge'.[52]

Having crafted his criteria for knowledge, al-Ghazali tells us that he scrutinized all his beliefs he thought were instances of such knowledge, and found that, initially, all that passed the conditions he set up were beliefs based on sense-data and self-evident truths (p. 64). He then thought that all subsequent beliefs must, therefore, be inferred from such truths to safeguard against error. But, as he reflected further, al-Ghazali explains that even beliefs based on sense-data and self-evident truths were not secure from doubt (ibid).

44   *Classical scholastic fideism in Islam*

First, he considers beliefs based on sense-data, the strongest of which, according to him, is sight. Al-Ghazali gives two examples where beliefs formed on the basis of what appears to be the case to our sight are wrong. We may, for instance, form a belief that a shadow we observe is motionless. But observation and reflection tells us that a shadow is always moving, however slowly, and is never completely at rest (ibid). Or we might, as al-Ghazali states in his second example, look at a star in the sky and believe it to be the size of a dinar, but geometrical proofs reveal that it is, in fact, larger than the earth in size (ibid). Several other cases can be conceived, says al-Ghazali, where beliefs formed based on sense-data are proved false by considerations based on reason. Clearly, then, beliefs formed based on sense-data may be doubted and therefore do not quality as instances of knowledge, according to al-Ghazali's criteria.

Next, al-Ghazali proceeds to consider beliefs based on reason, in particular self-evident truths. Perhaps beliefs based on truths such as 'Ten is more than three' or 'One and the same thing cannot be simultaneously affirmed and denied' are secure against doubt. Al-Ghazali gives a primary argument to doubt that confidence can be placed in such beliefs, followed by a secondary argument to consolidate his skepticism. The first argument is as follows: a person may be completely convinced that beliefs formed based on sense-data count as instances of knowledge, but have his conviction subsequently overturned when the faculty of reason reveals that such beliefs are not completely safe from error. Perhaps there is a faculty higher than that of reason which, if it were to emerge, would show the judgments of reason to be unreliable in much the same way that the faculty of reason sometimes shows judgments based on sense-data to be unreliable (p. 65). Al-Ghazali notes that he hesitated to accept the full force of this argument, until he reflected further and thought about what happens when we dream (ibid). He then entertains what he takes to be a second, more powerful argument, based on considerations related to dreaming, to doubt the self-evident truths of reason. When we are asleep and dream, we enter a state where we may hold certain beliefs with absolute conviction and not entertain any doubts about them. Upon waking up, however, we realize that what we thought was true (perhaps even with certainty), is groundless. What assurance do we have, then, that there isn't another possible state beyond our present state of being awake, where all our rational considerations would be seen as groundless? The Sufis, according to al-Ghazali, say that they have transcended to such a state: "For they allege that, in the states they experience when they concentrate inwardly and suspend sensation, they see phenomena which are not in accord with the normal data of reason" (pp. 65–66). Since this possibility cannot be ruled out, even self-evident truths are subject to doubt and hence beliefs based on them cannot fall under the rubric of 'sure and certain knowledge'. Against this skeptical conclusion, al-Ghazali explains that he had no possible reply, "since the objection could be refuted only by proof. But the only way to put together a proof was to combine primary cognitions. So if, as in my case, these were inadmissible, it was impossible to construct the proof" (p. 66).

Classical scholastic fideism in Islam   45

Having descended so deeply into the abyss of extreme skepticism, al-Ghazali gives us a brief account of what Muhammad Ali Khalidi calls his "fideist resolution."[53] Al-Ghazali writes,

> This malady [of extreme scepticism] was mysterious and it lasted for nearly two months. During that time, I was a skeptic in fact, but not in utterance and doctrine. At length God Most High cured me of that sickness. My soul regained its health and equilibrium and once again I accepted the self-evident data of reason and relied on them with safety and certainty. But that was not achieved by constructing a proof or putting together an argument. On the contrary, it was the effect of a light which God Most High cast into my breast. And that light is the key to most knowledge. Therefore, whoever thinks that the unveiling of truth depends on precisely formulated proofs has indeed straitened the broad mercy of God.
>
> (ibid)[54]

According to al-Ghazali, God had given him the assurance he needed that beliefs based on the self-evident truths of reason could be relied upon. After having given his readers an account and resolution of his crisis of radical skepticism, al-Ghazali enters into a discussion of truth-seekers and where the truth about religious matters is to be found.

3.2 Al-Ghazali on truth-seekers and the limits of reason

"When God Most High, of His kindness and abundant generosity, had cured me of this sickness [of radical skepticism]," writes al-Ghazali, "I was of the view that the categories of those seeking the truth were limited to four groups" (p. 67). He then provides us with the following taxonomy of these groups:

1   The *Mutakallimūn* ['Scholastic Theologians' engaging in *kalam*], who allege that they are men of independent judgment and reasoning.
2   The *Bātinites* ['Instructionists'], who claim to be the unique possessors of *al-ta'līm* [instruction] and the privileged recipients of knowledge acquired from the Infallible Imām.[55]
3   The Philosophers, who maintain that they are the men of logic and apodeictic demonstration.
4   The Sufis, who claim to be the familiars of the Divine Presence and the men of mystic vision and illumination (ibid).

Al-Ghazali maintains that this taxonomy is exhaustive; these are the only groups in which purported truth-seekers are to be found. Hence, "if the truth eludes them, there remains no hope of ever attaining it" (ibid). Having explained that he understood where he must look in order to find the truth concerning religious matters, al-Ghazali writes that he wasted no time at all in embarking on a thorough study of the views held by members belonging

46   *Classical scholastic fideism in Islam*

to each group. First, he studied *kalam*, second philosophy, third the views of the Batinites, and fourth the perspective of the Sufis (p. 68).

It is important to note here that, according to al-Ghazali, the only beliefs in which epistemic confidence was restored for him (as part of his fideist resolution), prior to his systematic investigation of the classes of truth-seekers, were those based on the self-evident truths of reason. Thus he states explicitly ('My soul regained its health and equilibrium and once again I accepted the self-evident data of reason and relied on them with safety and certainty'). Although al-Ghazali does not mention what he thought about beliefs based on sense-data during or after the resolution of his skeptical crisis, Khalidi makes a plausible point regarding this matter: "We can presume that ... his sensory beliefs [were also restored], since he would surely have needed them to get further in his intellectual quest."[56] Al-Ghazali's investigation of the classes of truth-seekers can thus be seen as being predicated on the following basic question: *Given that beliefs based on the self-evident truths of reason and also sense-data count as 'sure and certain' knowledge, how far is one able to proceed in acquiring 'sure and certain' knowledge regarding religious matters?*

First, al-Ghazali considers the *mutakallimun* and the science of *kalam*. After a careful study of this science, he tells us that he found it adequate for its own purposes, but not for his (p. 68). The aim of *kalam*, explains al-Ghazali, is "simply to conserve the creed of the orthodox for the orthodox and to guard it from the confusion introduced by the innovators" (ibid). Although God revealed a religious creed for His servants to follow, it became diseased with heresy through the works of Satan and the innovators. To safeguard the orthodox creed, God raised up a group of *mutakallimun* to "champion orthodoxy by a systematic discussion designed to disclose the deceptions introduced by the contriving innovators contrary to the traditional orthodoxy" (ibid). The *mutakallimun* did succeed in defending orthodoxy, but employed methods that did not begin from the self-evident truths of reason. Rather, the initial premises motivating their discourse were either uncritically accepted or else accepted by a simple derivation from the Qur'an and the prophetic traditions. Beginning, then, from revelation, the *mutakallimun* criticized their opponents for inconsistencies or logical absurdities that followed, given the generally agreed upon starting point of revelation for all parties in theological disputes (ibid). Although this is fine, it "is of little use in the case of one who admits nothing at all except the primary and self-evident truths," writes al-Ghazali. Thus, "*kalām* was not sufficient in my case, nor was it a remedy for the malady of which I was complaining" (ibid). I take it that what al-Ghazali means here is something like this. Having been cured of radical skepticism, he is prepared to concede the reliability of self-evident truths and sense-data but nothing more. Given that we can trust beliefs based on self-evident truths and sense-data, can the science of *kalam* take us to the point where beliefs about religious matters can qualify as sure and certain knowledge? The answer is 'no', because the practitioners of *kalam* begin with revelation as a given truth; they simply *assume*

Classical scholastic fideism in Islam 47

that the religious beliefs affiliated with revelation count as 'sure and certain' knowledge without providing the necessary epistemic justification for maintaining this stance. Because of this, *kalam* cannot satisfy al-Ghazali's quest for 'sure and certain' knowledge regarding religious matters, a quest that initially only admits the bare foundations of knowledge.

After having provided relatively mild criticisms of *kalam* in his brief examination of it, al-Ghazali advances to engage in a much lengthier, and harsher, discussion of philosophy. He tells us that he started studying philosophy after he had finished with *kalam* (p. 69). Confidently, al-Ghazali explains that none of what the Muslim thinkers of his time, including the *mutakallimun*, said about philosophy was accurate. Thus, he conducted a private study of the doctrines of the philosophers and this took him less than two years, after which he reflected on his findings for nearly a year (p. 70). During his study, he discovered two basic things – (1) the philosophers themselves fell into several categories and (2) the science of the philosophers included several divisions (ibid). Although there are boundaries to be drawn, one thing is very clear: "[t]o all of them, despite the multiplicity of categories, cleaves the stigma of unbelief and godlessness" (ibid).

The three basic divisions among the philosophers, according to al-Ghazali, are as follows – (1) 'materialists', (2) 'naturalists' and (3) 'theists' (p. 71). The materialists (*Al-dahriyyun*) are those ancient philosophers who were atheists, believing that the world had existed from eternity and hence had no need for a maker. They are "godless in the full sense of the term" (ibid). The naturalists (*Al-tabi'iyyun*) are those philosophers who devoted much study to the world of nature, and, having marveled at the wisdom of design in nature, were forced to admit the existence of a Creator God. They are, nevertheless, godless men too because they denied the afterlife and the Day of Judgment. "[B]asic faith is belief in God and the Last Day – and these men denied the Last Day, even though they believed in God and his attributes" (pp. 71–72). The theists (*Al-ilahiyyun*) include philosophers such as Socrates, Plato and Aristotle, who refuted some of the views of the materialists and naturalists. But even among this group of theist philosophers there was disagreement; Aristotle disassociated himself from both Plato and Socrates, having refuted some of the doctrines of his predecessors. Nevertheless, residual elements of unbelief and innovation remained in his philosophy. Thus, Aristotle, Plato and Socrates must be charged with unbelief, as well as those among the Muslim philosophers who follow him, such as Ibn Sina and al-Farabi. No one among the philosophers of the Muslim community transmitted Aristotle's philosophy to such a degree as Ibn Sina and al-Farabi. When we consider the Aristotelian philosophy that these two have transmitted to us, says al-Ghazali, we can divide it into three basic parts: "a part which must be branded as unbelief; a part which must be stigmatized as innovation; and a part which need not be repudiated at all" (p. 72). These three basic designations emerge within the six divisions present in the sciences of the philosophers, which are the (1) mathematical, (2) logical, (3) physical, (4) metaphysical, (5) political and (6) moral (ibid).

48   *Classical scholastic fideism in Islam*

Starting with the mathematical sciences, al-Ghazali explains that he has no in principle objection to them since "nothing in them entails denial or affirmation of religious matters" (p. 73). Nevertheless, mathematics may give rise to two evils. First, a person might mistakenly think that, because of the clarity of mathematical proofs, all the sciences of the philosophers have "the same lucidity and apodeictic solidity." Hence, he might be swayed by the ir-religiousness of the philosophers, thinking that their criticisms of religious belief rest on the same sort clarity and level of justification found in mathe-matical proofs (ibid). Second, an "ignorant friend of Islam" may think that advocating the Islamic religion entails a rejection of all the sciences of the philosophers. The reason this is dangerous is because it may lead a person to think that Islam is built on ignorance and that it has no regard for apodictic demonstration. Such a person may then become more attached to philosophy and more averse to Islam. To think that advocacy of Islam requires a denial of the mathematical sciences, warns al-Ghazali, is a "great crime" (p. 74).

After mathematics, al-Ghazali considers logic and confers a similar judgment regarding it; there is no in principle objection against the logical sciences because nothing in them "has anything to do with religion by way of negation and affirmation" (ibid). Still, logic too may give rise to some problems in the same manner as mathematics. A person who rejects the logical sciences may supply others with reason to hold the religion he is affil-iated with in low regard. Another problem (a charge that al-Ghazali repeats on several occasions throughout his works) is that the philosophers fail to satisfy their own conditions of apodictic demonstration in their discussions of metaphysical matters that have religious import. A person who studies logic and is impressed with its clarity may then erroneously think that the philosophers' criticisms and rejection of Islamic belief rest on successful logical demonstrations. Thus, such a person "will rush into unbelief even before reaching the metaphysical sciences [in his study]" (p. 75).

Next, al-Ghazali provides some brief remarks regarding the physical sciences, which involve "a study of the world of the heavens and their stars and of the sublunar world's simple bodies, such as water, air, earth, and fire, and composite bodies, such as animals, plants and minerals" (pp. 75–76). From the perspective of religion, there is no need to repudiate the science of physics, apart from what he has already discussed in the *Incoherence*.[57] The basic point that those who study the physical sciences should understand is that nature has no power in and of itself; it is completely subject to the power of God (p. 76).

After having given us his assessment of three out of the six divisions of phi-losophy, al-Ghazali turns to metaphysics, where he notes that "most of the philosophers' errors are found" (ibid). The fundamental problem with the phi-losophers' treatment of metaphysics is that they cannot satisfy their own criteria for apodictic demonstration. Their errors in religious matters can be reduced to twenty propositions, three of which constitute unbelief and the remaining sev-enteen are innovations. Here, al-Ghazali refers his readers to the *Incoherence*, which was written to "refute their doctrine on these twenty questions" (ibid).

Classical scholastic fideism in Islam   49

Al-Ghazali's briefest remarks in his discussion of the divisions of philosophy are reserved for the political sciences, which he mentions after metaphysics. The sum of what the philosophers say regarding political matters "comes down to administrative maxims concerned with secular affairs and the government of rulers." But these they simply borrowed from what God revealed in scriptures and from the aphorisms of the predecessors of the prophets (ibid).

Finally, al-Ghazali considers the moral sciences, where what the philosophers have to say "comes down to listing the qualities and habits of the soul, and recording their generic and specific kinds, and the way to cultivate the good ones and combat the bad" (ibid). He asserts that here the philosophers simply borrowed the ideas of the Sufis, but mixed them with their own doctrines. This results in two evils, one in the case of a person who accepts the ethical teaching of the philosophers and the other in the case of a person who rejects it (p. 78). The evil in the case of the person who rejects it occurs when the ethical teaching of the philosophers is rejected in its totality just because it comes from the philosophers. The problem here, notes al-Ghazali, is that truth will also be discarded with falsehood. The intelligent man should be willing to discern truth in the sayings of the philosophers on ethical matters from their falsehood, in a manner similar to the money-changer who is capable of carefully withdrawing genuine gold coins from the sack of the trickster who carries both genuine and counterfeit coins (p. 79). Because the ethical teachings of the philosophers have truth in them mixed along with falsehood, evil may also occur when a person completely accepts what the philosophers have to say on ethical matters (p. 80). To avoid the deceit and danger posed by these two evils, "the ears of men must be protected from the farrago of [the philosophers'] sayings [on ethical matters]" (p. 81).

After having discussed the sixth and final division of philosophy, al-Ghazali states that he has said all he wishes to say about its "evil and mischief" (ibid). And, at the start of the section where he starts to discuss the doctrines and views of the Batinites, he provides the following conclusion:

> When I had finished with the science of philosophy – having fully mastered and understood it and pinpointed its errors – I knew that philosophy was also inadequate to satisfy my aim fully. I also realized that reason alone is incapable of fully grasping all problems or of getting to the heart of all difficulties.
>
> (pp. 81–82)

But why exactly is philosophy unable to satisfy al-Ghazali's quest for truth about religious matters? In his discussion of the subject in the *Deliverance*, al-Ghazali explains, as we have seen, what is and is not acceptable in philosophy from an Islamic point of view. He does not, however, elaborate in detail why the discipline cannot in principle aid him in his quest for truth about religious matters. Still, al-Ghazali makes it clear that the basis of his repudiation of the philosophers is their failure to adequately demonstrate what they say

50 *Classical scholastic fideism in Islam*

about religious matters, particularly those matters that are in the domain of metaphysics. But then perhaps the reason why the philosophers have failed in this regard is because philosophical investigation about such matters cannot hope to succeed. As Stephen Menn explains, al-Ghazali "has serious criticisms of the philosophers. He believes ... that many of their alleged demonstrations are not real demonstrations, and that *their methods* are incapable of resolving many fundamental questions about God and the world."[58] Several authors have noted that al-Ghazali appears to anticipate Kant's criticisms of philosophical speculation about metaphysical matters, such as the existence of God, the freedom of the will, the immortality of the soul, etc.[59]

After having discussed the views of the *mutakallimun* and the philosophers, al-Ghazali's discussion of truth-seekers who utilize rational argument in discussions of religious matters comes to an end. The remaining two groups – the Batinites and the Sufis – do not rely on rational argumentation in order to obtain religious knowledge. The former group relies on the authority of an infallible Imam, whereas the latter group resorts to a mystical apprehension of religious truths. At this point in al-Ghazali's discussion of truth-seekers, we can see how he would object to those who are interested in philosophically investigating Islamic belief. Any adequate epistemology of religious belief will begin only with beliefs based on the self-evident truths of reason and sense-data. The reason that *kalam* cannot give us an adequate religious epistemology is because the *mutakallimun* begin with revelation as their starting point and hence admit more than the basic foundations of knowledge. The problem with *falsifah*, on the other hand, is that the philosophers are unable to reason their way to any definite conclusions regarding God and the world, even though they may admit only religiously neutral truths in their initial premises.

Because philosophical considerations cannot provide the foundations necessary to ground the rationality of fundamental Islamic beliefs according to al-Ghazali, one could argue that his views, if accepted, lead to a rejection of philosophical investigation as a means of determining the truth of Islamic doctrine. But this does not necessarily mean that Islamic beliefs are groundless. On the contrary, they may have a nonrational foundation. After considering *kalam* and *falsifah* in the *Deliverance*, al-Ghazali proceeds to discuss the Batinites, who claim to be recipients of certain knowledge about religious matters through an infallible Imam and without recourse to rational speculation. He forcefully criticizes their position, maintaining that "there is no substance to their views and no force to their argument" (p. 83). For our purposes, there is no need to consider al-Ghazali's critical discussion of the Batinites. Having argued that neither the *mutakallimun*, nor the philosophers, nor the Batinites can provide him with sure and certain knowledge about religious matters, al-Ghazali turns to the fourth and final group on his list of truth-seekers – the Sufis (p. 89). He explains that he found the sure and certain knowledge he was seeking regarding religious matters through a nonrational apprehension of religious truth by following the Sufi path.

In his discussion of the Sufi path, al-Ghazali offers a number of arguments in favor of Sufism that play an auxiliary role in supporting his rejection of philosophy as being able to provide the epistemic basis for Islamic belief. It will therefore be useful to consider these arguments alongside al-Ghazali's more direct criticisms of philosophical investigations about religious matters.

3.3 Going beyond reason: Al-Ghazali on the Sufis and Al-Dhawq ('fruitional experience')

The unique way (*tariqa*) of the Sufis, explains al-Ghazali, is realized only by combining theory and practice (p. 89). Theoretically speaking, the fundamental endeavor of the Sufis is to purify the soul so that all that remains in the heart is remembrance of God. He informs us that he learnt this, along with other aspects of the theory behind Sufism, by studying the books of the Sufi masters (p. 90). But there was more to learn:

> [I]t became clear to me that their most distinctive characteristic is something that can be attained, not by study, but rather by fruitional experience [*Al-Dhawq*] and the state of ecstasy [*Al-hāl*] and "the exchange of [moral] qualities." How great a difference there is between your *knowing* the definitions and causes and conditions of health and satiety and your *being* healthy and sated! And how great a difference there is between your knowing the definition of drunkenness – viz. that it is a term denoting a state resulting from the predominance of vapors which rise from the stomach to the centers of thought – and your actually being drunk! Indeed, a drunken man, while he is drunk, does not know the definition and concept of drunkenness and he has no knowledge of it. But a physician knows the definition and elements of drunkenness, though he is experiencing no actual drunkenness. So also, when a physician is ill, he knows the definition and causes of health and the remedies which procure it, though he is then actually bereft of health. Similarly, too, there is a difference between your knowing the true nature and conditions and causes of asceticism and your actually practicing asceticism and personally shunning the things of this world.
>
> (ibid)

In this important passage, al-Ghazali points out that the most 'distinctive characteristic' of the Sufis is attained by *dhawq*, being in a state of ecstasy and the exchanging of moral qualities.[60] Literally, the word *dhawq* in Arabic means 'taste' with connotations of enjoyment or intoxication, but it also refers to a kind of immediate perception or cognition.[61] *Dhawq*, or 'fruitional experience', forms a key concept in al-Ghazali's discussion of Sufism, as it does in other medieval philosophical discussions on religious knowledge.[62] In the passage from the *Deliverance* just quoted above, al-Ghazali uses the

52   *Classical scholastic fideism in Islam*

concept to point out that there is a marked difference between theoretical knowledge of, say, health on one hand, and, on the other, knowledge through an intimate awareness of being healthy.[63] Similarly, this distinction also exists between theoretical understanding of asceticism and actually practicing it (p. 90). Having come to realize this distinction, al-Ghazali writes that he subsequently took up the path of the Sufis after learning all he could about the theory surrounding their practice:

> ... I had learned all I could [about the Sufis] by way of theory. There remained, then, only what was attainable, not by hearing and study, but by fruitional experience and actually engaging in the way. From the sciences which I had practiced and the methods which I had followed in my inquiry into the two kinds of knowledge, revealed and rational, I had already acquired a sure and certain faith in God Most High, in the prophetic mediation of revelation, and in the Last Day. These three fundamentals of our Faith had become deeply rooted in my soul, not because of any specific, precisely formulated proofs, but because of reasons and circumstances and experiences too many to list in detail.
>
> (pp. 90–91)

Given the brevity of this passage, and the evasive nature of the closing comment, it is somewhat difficult to understand and articulate just how al-Ghazali had acquired 'sure and certain faith' in the fundamental beliefs of Islam. What seems reasonably clear, though, is that certainty regarding these beliefs was secured nonrationally for him. For, not only does he tell us in this passage that rational proofs did not play a role in securing the truth of essential Islamic beliefs in his soul, he has already explained earlier in the *Deliverance* why the methods of *kalam* and *falsifah* failed to satisfy (and *could not* satisfy) his quest for truth concerning religious matters. Since al-Ghazali informs us about his acquisition of the fundamentals of Islamic belief within the context of discussing the concept of *dhawq*, it seems plausible to think that he acquired certainty regarding these beliefs through fruitional experience.

What follows after the previous passage I have quoted from the *Deliverance* is a fairly detailed account of a *religious* crisis that al-Ghazali underwent, involving an agonizing conflict between worldly passions on one hand and the aspirations for God and the hereafter on the other (p. 91ff). It is clear from reading this account that al-Ghazali entered it as a Muslim, already believing in God, Revelation and the Last Day. His main concern at the outset of this particular crisis, he tells us, was to attain "beatitude in the afterlife" and avoid "falling into the Fire [of Hell]" (ibid). What this must mean, then, is that his earlier *epistemological* crisis must have been resolved prior to the onset of this religious one. Al-Ghazali gives us an account of his religious crisis within the section of the *Deliverance* in which he discusses the Sufis. These two points of discussion are related because after vacillating between "the contending pull of worldly desires and the appeals of the afterlife for

Classical scholastic fideism in Islam 53

about six months" (p. 92), he tells us that he left Baghdad to become a wandering Sufi and to follow their ways in an attempt to secure his salvation.

What prompted al-Ghazali to follow the Sufi way? A reasonable suggestion, it seems to me, is that al-Ghazali had resolved his epistemological crisis regarding the fundamentals of Islamic belief through *dhawq* or fruitional experience and, having come to learn about this sort of experience more fully in Sufism, sought to apply it further to resolve his religious crisis. After ten years of pursuing the path of the Sufis, he tells us what he learnt:

> I knew with certainty that the Sufis are those who uniquely follow the way to God Most High, their mode of life is the best of all, their way the most direct of ways, and their ethic the purest. Indeed, were one to combine the insight of the intellectuals, the wisdom of the wise, and the lore of the scholars versed in the mysteries of revelation in order to change a single item of Sufi conduct and ethic and to replace it with something better, no way to do so would be found! For all their motions and quiescences, exterior and interior, are learned from the light of the niche of prophecy. And beyond the light of prophecy there is no light on earth from which illumination can be obtained.
>
> (p. 94)

Here, after lavishing the Sufis with praise, al-Ghazali draws a link between *dhawq* and prophecy, which he elaborates upon later in the *Deliverance*. He writes that "[w]hat became clear to [him] of necessity from practicing [the] Way [of the Sufis] was the true nature and special character of prophecy" (p. 96). After finishing his discussion on Sufism, al-Ghazali briefly elaborates on, and offers arguments for, the reality of the phenomenon of prophecy. Since prophecy is connected to his discussion of Sufism and *dhawq*, it will be useful to consider what he has to say regarding it.

3.4 Al-Ghazali's arguments in favor of prophecy

Al-Ghazali starts his discussion of prophecy by telling us that "man's essence, in his original condition, is created in blank simplicity without any information about the 'worlds' of God Most High" (p. 96). He explains that we learn about things that exist in a 'world' through perception and that there are different types of perception, each of which is made for us by God for a particular world. 'Worlds', for al-Ghazali, refer to "the categories of existing things" (ibid). The first type of perception that God creates in us is touch, by which we can perceive things such as heat and cold, wetness and dryness, and so on; but what we can perceive through touch is, of course, limited. We cannot, for instance, perceive colors and sounds through touch. Next, God creates in us our sense of sight, through which we can perceive colors and shapes. Third, we are given the sense of hearing in order to perceive sounds and tones. After this, God creates the sense of taste. These

54   *Classical scholastic fideism in Islam*

four types of perception allow us to perceive things in "the world of the sensibles" (pp. 96–97). Around the age of seven, God gives man 'discernment', allowing him to perceive things beyond the world of the sensibles. And after this, God creates the intellect for man, which allows him to perceive the classification of beings (ibid).

Thus far, al-Ghazali's general account of the various cognitive faculties that we possess appears relatively uncontroversial (if we set aside his account of the *order* in which we acquire these faculties, as well as his theological explanation for their origin). According to al-Ghazali, these cognitive faculties are not the only ones that we have:

> Beyond the stage of intellect there is another stage. In this another eye is opened, by which man sees the hidden, and what will take place in the future, and other things, from which the intellect is as far removed as the power of discernment is from the perception of intelligibles and the power of sensation is from things perceived by discernment. And just as one able only to discern, if presented with things perceptible to the intellect, would reject them and consider them as outlandish, so some men endowed with intellect have rejected the things perceptible to the prophetic power and considered them wildly improbable. That is the very essence of ignorance! For such a man has no supporting reason except that it is a stage he himself has not attained and for him it does not exist: so he supposes that it does not exist in itself.
>
> (p. 97)

Here, the stage to which al-Ghazali refers that supersedes the intellect is *nubuwwa* (prophecy).[64] Together with his explanation of prophecy, he offers an argument against those who are quick to dismiss the possibility of its occurrence. Just as one who has only reached the stage of discernment and not further would reject things that are perceptible only to the intellect, so too would a person who has not progressed past the stage of the intellect reject things that are perceptible only to prophetic power. But if the former move is absurd, then, by parity of reasoning, so is the latter. Our attitude towards someone who is skeptical of claims about perceiving certain things through prophetic power should be similar to our reaction to, say, a very young child whose perception is confined to the world of the sensibles and who is unable to understand claims about things perceivable only through discernment and the intellect.

Now, someone might be skeptical about the phenomenon of prophecy in a way similar to the case of a blind man who would be skeptical if he were told about colors and shapes, not having heard about them before (ibid). But, says al-Ghazali, God has given us a sample of prophetic power through sleeping and dreaming, "[f]or the sleeper perceives the unknown that will take place, either plainly, or in the guise of an image the meaning of which is disclosed by interpretation" (ibid). A person who never had the experience of dreaming would deny this, thinking that the scope of reliable perception

Classical scholastic fideism in Islam 55

is limited to our ordinary sensory powers (pp. 97–98). But, as a matter of fact, one can show such a person to be wrong through "factual experience and observation" (p. 98).

Al-Ghazali maintains that doubts about prophecy are of three types – (1) doubts about its possibility, (2) doubts about its actual existence and (3) doubts about prophecy belonging to a specific individual (ibid). He addresses the first and second doubts together by providing an argument for (2), basing this move on the following logical principle: if something *exists*, then *a fortiori* it must be *possible for it to exist*.[65] What evidence is there, then, that the phenomenon of prophecy is real? Al-Ghazali provides the following answer to this question:

> [T]he proof of its *existence* is the existence in the world of knowledge which could not conceivably be obtained by the intellect alone – such as the knowledge of medicine and of astronomy. For whoever examines such knowledge knows of necessity that it can be obtained only by a divine inspiration and a special help from God Most High, and that there is no empirical way to it.
>
> (ibid)

If this is indeed the case, then, based on the aforementioned principle, "it is clearly within the bounds of possibility that a way exists to grasp these things which the intellect does not normally grasp" (ibid). Perceiving things that are beyond the intellect is but one aspect of prophetic power. It has many other properties, and al-Ghazali points out that what he has mentioned is just "a drop from its sea" (ibid). The additional properties of prophecy can be perceived only through fruitional experience by following the way of Sufism (p. 99). Still, al-Ghazali thinks that the examples he has given suffice to show that it is a real phenomenon.

As for the third type of doubt concerning prophecy, doubt regarding whether it belongs to a specific individual, certainty regarding an individual's claim to be a true prophet can come only through acquaintance with his circumstances, either by way of personal observation or testimony (ibid). We do this, al-Ghazali writes, with respect to other areas of expertise, such as medicine and jurisprudence, recognizing people as physicians and jurisprudents by observing their circumstances. For instance, we know that al-Shafi'i was a jurisprudent and that Galen was a physician based on our knowledge of jurisprudence and medicine and by studying their works (ibid). Similarly, when one studies the Qur'an and the prophetic traditions, one will come to know that the Prophet Muhammad had attained "the loftiest level of prophecy" (ibid). This fact can also be confirmed by sampling what the Prophet said regarding acts of worship and their effect on purifying the heart. After putting into practice what he said, and having confirmed it several thousand times over, one will "[acquire] a necessary knowledge [about the truth of Muhammad's Prophethood] which will be indisputable" (p. 100).

56 *Classical scholastic fideism in Islam*

This, according to al-Ghazali, is the proper way to acquire sure and certain knowledge about prophecy – by studying the Qur'an and the prophetic traditions and by putting into practice what Muhammad said. One should not resort to rational proofs and apologetic arguments based on miracles to confirm prophecy, because doubts may be raised about the occurrence of miracles as well as about the mode of apologetic argumentation (ibid).

Al-Ghazali concludes his discussion of prophecy by stating that fruitional experience, a concept that plays an important role in his defense of the reality of prophetic phenomena, "is found only in the way of the Sufis" (ibid). The rest of the *Deliverance* mentions matters which need not concern us for present purposes. What is clear from reading al-Ghazali's full account in this work is that, by the end of his journey as a Sufi, both his epistemological and religious crises appear to have been resolved. Al-Ghazali tells us that after having returned from his spiritual journey, his desire was to impart authentic religious knowledge and to reform other people (p. 107). His motivation came from "a faith as certain as direct vision that there is no might for [him] and no power save in God, the Sublime, the Mighty" (ibid).

If al-Ghazali is correct, there is a nonrational or supra-rational epistemological state that one can enter in order to obtain religious knowledge. Thus, there is simply no need for a philosophical investigation in order to acquire knowledge about religious matters. In looking at al-Ghazali's arguments in favor of Sufism, *dhawq* and prophecy, we can see how they serve to provide additional motivation for rejecting the application of the philosophical method to Islamic belief.

This, then, is my summary presentation of al-Ghazali's scholastic fideism, done, I hope, as charitably as possible.[66] What follows next is my assessment of its worth and merit as a case against philosophically investigating the Islamic religion.

4. *Contra* Al-Ghazali: a defense of philosophizing about religious (Islamic) belief

Perhaps the first place to begin in responding to al-Ghazali's criticisms of philosophy is to note the common assertion that the 'Proof of Islam' had 'refuted philosophy' is simply not true, *even if one accepts all of his criticisms*. Several points can be raised here. For one thing, al-Ghazali's criticisms of the philosophers in the *Incoherence of the Philosophers*, his main work on the subject of philosophy, are not criticisms of philosophy *per se* but rather *criticisms pointing out the failure to philosophize properly*. As we saw, his primary complaint against the philosophers is that their heretical views do not satisfy the criteria of logical demonstration they themselves set up. In the *Incoherence*, al-Ghazali explicitly endorses logic as an instrument and engages in philosophical reasoning to show on their own turf that the philosophers are wrong in subscribing to their unorthodox views regarding religious matters. Furthermore, in his *Moderation in Belief*, he

Classical scholastic fideism in Islam   57

holds rational argumentation in high regard, even though he thinks that its function and scope is limited, and he censures those who wish to dismiss it altogether. And in *The Deliverance from Error*, he makes some more important points and concessions about the worth of philosophy. Although, according to al-Ghazali, some philosophical beliefs do constitute out-and-out unbelief, there are other beliefs that merit the less serious label of heresy and yet others that are perfectly acceptable from an Islamic point of view. The reason this is the case is because philosophy itself, as he explains, is divided into six categories of mathematics, logic, physics (or the natural sciences), metaphysics, politics and the moral sciences (or ethics). Most of these divisions within philosophy, when approached cautiously, are fine. It is in the metaphysical sciences, an area that forms only a *part* of philosophy, where most of the philosophers err. To claim, then, that al-Ghazali 'refuted philosophy' is just not true.

It remains true, however, that al-Ghazali provides a number of considerations that may be taken as presenting a case against the feasibility of philosophical investigations of Islamic belief. This case can be broken down into two main components – (1) al-Ghazali's criticisms of the methods of philosophical argumentation as exemplified by *kalam* and *falsifah* and (2) al-Ghazali's arguments in favor of Sufism and prophecy, which supplement (1).

4.1 Reply to Al-Ghazali's criticisms of applying philosophical methodology to Islamic belief

The basic structure of al-Ghazali's argument against applying philosophical methodology to Islamic belief is as follows: first, he explains that what is required is 'sure and certain' knowledge regarding religious matters and constructs criteria under which Islamic belief can meet the conditions for such knowledge to obtain. Second, he argues that philosophy (along with *kalam* and the views of the Batinites) cannot show that Islamic belief constitutes sure and certain knowledge according to his criteria. From this, he concludes that philosophy is unable to show that Islamic belief can be justifiably held. The implication here is that a philosophical investigation of Islam is not a viable or beneficial endeavor. This is not a good argument. Although many objections can be raised against it, I shall limit myself to a selection that will show the argument has little force.

(a) The nature of reflective inquiry given the problem of religious diversity: Towards the beginning of the *Deliverance*, al-Ghazali tells us that reflection on the problem of diversity in beliefs about religion gave him reason to reflect on his own religious beliefs and instilled in him a desire to go beyond *taqlid*. This sounds like a reasonable thing to think. Since many different and often inconsistent beliefs are held by people based on *taqlid* (e.g., the Muslim belief that Allah exists is inconsistent with the belief of classical Buddhists

58   *Classical scholastic fideism in Islam*

that no god exists), it is understandable how, upon reflection, one may desire to sift through such beliefs to try and discern truth from falsehood.

But, for al-Ghazali, the desire to seek truth in the face of religious diversity expresses itself in a very specific and stringent sense. Given the problem of diversity in beliefs about religion, he makes two basic claims – (1) *all* beliefs that one holds must constitute *knowledge* and, moreover, (2) for a person S to know that p requires the belief that p to be 'infallibly justified' for S (that is to say, the belief that p must pass al-Ghazali's criteria for knowledge, as specified in the *Deliverance*). I will address the first of these two basic claims here, dealing with the second one later below.

The first difficulty with al-Ghazali's discussion of the problem of religious diversity is that reflection on this problem gives us no reason to think that we must check *all* our beliefs to make sure that they constitute knowledge. There are many beliefs we hold that have nothing to do with religious matters. Consider, as two examples, our belief that food and water are required for human life or the belief that heat from the sun provides warmth on earth. Now, we do, as a matter of fact, regard these beliefs as instances of knowledge, but it is hard to see how the *motivation to check* whether these beliefs are items of knowledge could come about through reflection on disagreement in religious matters. For, one could rightly ask, what do such beliefs have to do with religion? Al-Ghazali gives us no reason to think disagreement in religious matters imposes a universal requirement on us to check that all the beliefs we hold are also instances of knowledge.

A sympathetic proponent of al-Ghazali's position might modify his original claim and maintain that disagreement in religious matters imposes on us a restricted requirement to scrutinize all beliefs about *religion* held based on *taqlid* to see whether they constitute knowledge. Here too, though, there are problems. Granted that disagreement may give one reason to go beyond *taqlid* when considering beliefs about religion, it does not follow that the only recourse is to make sure that the beliefs under question constitute *knowledge*. One might think that the choice here is either to continue holding the beliefs under question based on *taqlid* or else check them to see whether they constitute knowledge. But there is a third option that falls somewhere between the two. One could try to go beyond *taqlid* but not as far as trying to secure knowledge, by making sure that beliefs about religion are *justifiably* held. Let me elaborate. It is generally agreed by epistemologists that *knowledge* and *justified belief*, although conceptually related, are not synonymous. As Robert Audi explains,

> As closely associated knowledge and justified belief are, there is a major difference. If I know that something is so, then it is *true*, whereas I can justifiedly [*sic*] believe something that is false. If a normally reliable friend tricked me into believing something false, say that he has lost my car keys, I could justifiedly [*sic*] believe that he has lost them even if it were not true. We may not assume, then, that everything we learn about justified belief applies to knowledge.[67]

Classical scholastic fideism in Islam 59

Since a distinction exists between knowledge and justified belief, one may ask why, in light of disagreement about religious matters, the former is required instead of the latter?

Suppose I grow up as an orthodox Jew, acquiring all of my religious beliefs on the basis of *taqlid*. Suppose also that, at a certain point, I begin to reflect on this and realize that many other people from different religions, such as Muslims and Christians, hold their respective beliefs (many of which are inconsistent with mine) based on *taqlid* as well. Considering this, I might try to see whether the beliefs about Judaism that I hold can be justified on the basis of evidence and argument. I might, for example, look at the available evidence supporting the historicity of the Jewish account of God's revelation at Mount Sinai. Then, I might try to compare this evidence with the evidence cited by Muslims for thinking that the Archangel Gabriel revealed the Qur'an to Muhammad as well as the evidence cited by Christians in favor of the reality of the Resurrection. Finally, I might conclude that my commitment to orthodox Judaism is justified, since (according to my assessment) the evidence favors Jewish claims significantly more than the claims of Islam and Christianity. Suppose I can do all this and feel that I have reached a satisfactory resolve after having reflected on my religious beliefs that were initially based on *taqlid*. Why wouldn't this be good enough? Why would I need to go *further* to ensure that the beliefs under question constituted *knowledge*? Al-Ghazali doesn't really provide answers to such questions.

One might reply here that, with a *justified belief* that *p*, there is always the risk that *p* is false whereas *knowing* that *p* guarantees that *p* is true. And, one may plausibly continue, knowledge is preferable to justified belief, since the former guarantees truth while the latter does not. Even if this is granted, my point remains. Why must one attempt to go beyond holding justified beliefs about religious matters? Given reflection on *taqlid* and disagreements in religion, knowledge may be preferable to justified belief; no argument is provided by al-Ghazali, however, for thinking that the pursuit of knowledge in such a situation is mandatory.

(b) Does religious (Islamic) commitment require knowledge about religious (Islamic) claims? In thinking about what I have said above in (a), one might wonder whether there is something about being a committed Muslim or a person of religious faith in general that requires one to treat one's religious beliefs as items of knowledge. Perhaps al-Ghazali thinks that there is, based either on an understanding of Islamic faith specifically or the nature of religious commitment in general.

Let me consider Islamic faith first. Most people take the concept of faith in an Islamic (and Qur'anic) context to mean the Arabic word *iman*, which comes from the verb *amana*. As Jane I. Smith notes, the word *iman* is "most commonly understood as faith."[68] The verb *amana* means 'to be secure' or 'to put trust' in something. Thus, to have faith (*iman*) in God is to *trust* in God.[69] Does the act of trust require knowledge? It is not at all clear that it

60   *Classical scholastic fideism in Islam*

does. Indeed, there appears to be something implicit in our common understanding of trust that sees the concept predicated on a *lack* of knowledge. If I *know* that you will repay the money I lent you, then it does seem somewhat odd to say that I *trust* you will do this. Still, even if trust and knowledge are *compatible*, it certainly isn't clear that trust *entails* knowledge. If this is correct, then to have faith (in an Islamic context) does not *require* knowledge, even if such faith is *compatible* with it. So, it seems that al-Ghazali, or any sympathizer with his position, cannot straightforwardly appeal to the concept of faith in Islam in order to justify the view that knowledge is compulsory for Islamic commitment.

What, though, about the nature of religious commitment, broadly construed? Might there be something in the nature of such commitment that requires knowledge of religious claims? Many religious thinkers have maintained that authentic religious commitment has to be *wholehearted.* Let us suppose that this is true. One might then argue on the basis of this supposition that wholehearted religious commitment requires *certainty.* For, one might aver, wholehearted religious commitment is not possible if one is not certain about the religious claims that one is committed to. If there is a degree of uncertainty about the religious claims one entertains, then there will be an accompanying degree of *tentativeness* in religious commitment. Since tentative religious commitment does not *ex hypothesi* constitute a commitment that is authentic, one requires certainty in order to avoid tentativeness and have an authentic religious commitment. And this certainty can be provided only if one has knowledge of the relevant religious claims.

The argument just proposed is not convincing. Two independent lines of criticism can be offered against it.

(i) One difficulty with the argument is that it is not obvious knowledge is necessary for the *kind* of certainty that one might require for authentic religious commitment; that is, it appears possible to have a kind of certainty that is not *epistemic.* Some epistemologists have made a distinction between *psychological* certainty and *propositional* certainty.[70] The former, as Audi explains, refers to "great confidence of the truth of what one believes."[71] The latter, on the other hand, concerns "certainty a proposition has when there are extremely strong grounds for it, grounds that guarantee its truth."[72] When psychological certainty is combined with propositional certainty, then, according to some thinkers, knowledge constituted by justified belief in the truth of a proposition refers to a situation of *epistemic certainty.*[73] Since the notion of psychological certainty is embedded in but distinct from that of epistemic certainty, might it not be possible to enter into religious commitment wholeheartedly while being *psychologically* but not *epistemically* certain about the relevant religious claims? Or, to make this concern into a general question, might it be possible to have great confidence in the truth of a proposition while also maintaining that whatever grounds there are in favor of it do not *guarantee* its truth? There seem to be some reasons to answer in the affirmative to these questions.

Classical scholastic fideism in Islam 61

One reason is that the grounds in favor of a proposition may be *strong enough* to render belief in it *psychologically* certain, even if these grounds do not *guarantee* its truth. The architecture of human reason is not so finely calibrated that psychological certainty is *directly* proportional to its propositional counterpart. Often, when the grounds that point to the truth of a proposition reach a certain threshold in strength, we afford belief in that proposition psychological certainty. This can happen when grounds that are not truth-conductive (or 'nonevidential') influence the beliefs we hold, such as our desires.

Here is an example to illustrate the point. Suppose Jane suspects that her husband, Robert, was cheating on her last Saturday with a certain woman. She tries to uncover evidence to find out what he did that day and learns that, on the contrary, there are very good reasons to think Robert did *not* cheat on her. Several of Robert's friends offer independent testimony to Jane that he was playing golf with them all day last Saturday. She learns that the woman she thought was involved with Robert was actually out of the country that Saturday. She also learns that the strands of blonde hair on Robert's jacket (Jane is a brunette), which gave rise to the initial suspicion, actually belong to the maid who cleaned the house recently when no one was around. In this case, Jane has strong grounds for supposing that Robert did not cheat on her, even though they do not guarantee this. And although it is *possible* that she is wrong (perhaps this is all an elaborate hoax designed to throw her off track), she believes with psychological certainty that her husband did not cheat on her last Saturday. Apart from the strong evidence she has to support this, she also factors in her *emotions* and *feelings* for Robert (after all, he is her husband). She *wants* to believe that he is faithful, and this, along with the strong evidence she possesses, makes belief in Robert's fidelity (at least on the day in question!) *psychologically* but not *epistemically* certain for her.

In this kind of case, it seems that belief in the truth of a proposition can be psychologically certain, even if unaccompanied by epistemic certainty. Similarly, it seems quite reasonable to maintain that a person can be psychologically certain about the truth of a religious claim even if she lacks epistemic certainty about the religious proposition involved. For instance, a person might gather evidence in favor of the claim that there is a God and this evidence might provide grounds that strongly support, but do not guarantee the truth of, the proposition that God exists. Nevertheless, since this person is (we may suppose in considering this example) deeply immersed in a theistic tradition, various nonevidential causes (e.g., habitual involvement in certain religious practices) may significantly influence the confidence of her belief in God's existence to render it psychologically certain for her.

Indeed, psychological certainty may sometimes be associated with a belief without the involvement of *any* evidential considerations. Even when one lacks evidence to support the truth of a proposition, one may nevertheless come to be in a state of psychological certainty based on grounds other than those that are truth-conducive. Consider again the example of a

62   *Classical scholastic fideism in Islam*

person attempting to acquire supporting evidence for God's existence. Let us suppose that such a person fails to find evidence for thinking that God exists and, upon being urged to enter into theistic religious commitment, complains in the manner of Pascal's interlocutor in the famous 'Wager Argument':

> Yes, but my hands are tied and I cannot speak a word. I am being forced to wager and I am not free, they will not let me go. And I am made in such a way that I cannot believe. So what do you want me to do?[74]

In response, Pascal famously states:

> … concentrate not on convincing yourself by increasing the number of proofs of God but on diminishing your passions. You want to find faith and you do not know the way? You want to cure yourself of unbelief and you ask for remedies? Learn from those who have been bound like you, and who now wager all they have. They are people who know the road you want to follow and have been cured of the affliction of which you want to be cured. Follow the way by which they began: by behaving just as if they believed, taking holy water, having masses said, etc. That will make you believe quite naturally, and according to your animal reactions.[75]

Here, Pascal's interlocutor complains that he cannot *directly* acquire the belief that there is a God. In response, Pascal argues that, rather than trying to seek evidence ('proofs'), this belief can be acquired *indirectly* by living the religious life ('taking holy water, having masses said, etc.'). True, this case concerns *acquiring* a belief, not having *psychological certainty* regarding it. But one can see how Pascal's example can be extended to make it relevant. A person who *acts as if* God exists may not only come to acquire the belief that there is a God but may also eventually believe this with certainty after deep and sustained immersion in the religious life.

William James, in his famous essay 'The Will to Believe', lists several belief-forming grounds that are not truth-conducive and explains that these are part of our 'willing nature'.[76] By our 'willing nature', says James, he means

> … not … only such deliberate volitions as may have set up habits of belief that we cannot now escape from, - I mean all such factors of belief as fear and hope, prejudice and passion, imitation and partisanship, the circumpressure of our caste and set. As a matter of fact we find ourselves believing, we hardly know how or why.[77]

What James says here appears to be correct. Our 'willing nature' clearly does give rise to several beliefs that each of us have. Many cultural and religious beliefs that people have, for example, do have their origin in 'imitation and partisanship, the circumpressure of our caste and set'. Our 'willing

Classical scholastic fideism in Islam 63

nature' also has an influence on our preexisting beliefs. A certain cultural belief, such as not trusting foreigners as completely as locals, may be held fervently because of 'prejudice and passion', even when one recognizes that there is no good evidence to support it.

It seems to me, then, that psychological certainty about beliefs, including religious beliefs, may be acquired without truth-conducive grounds and *a fortiori* without truth-conducive grounds that guarantee their truth. Hence, psychological certainty may be obtained without knowledge or epistemic certainty. If psychological certainty is adequate for entering into religious commitment wholeheartedly, then we can see how such commitment can hold even when knowledge or epistemic certainty is not involved.

(ii) Here is another argument that can be given against the view that one requires knowledge of wholehearted religious commitment. The success of this argument is unaffected by the preceding discussion on certainty as a requirement for such commitment. Suppose that a person seeks evidence in favor of the theistic claim that God exists. He discovers evidence that, although not *guaranteeing* that there is a God, shows this claim to be at least as probable as its negation. Based on this evidence, he decides to enter into theistic religious commitment. Now, those who defend the view that knowledge is necessary for wholehearted religious commitment may argue that probabilistic evidence will never be able to rule out the possibility of error. Because of this, they may argue, the person who believes that God exists based on evidence that makes the truth of this claim only probable (p) will realize that there is a possibility of error ($1 - p$); therefore, it will be understood that there is a certain *risk* involved. But one cannot, the argument may run, enter into religious commitment wholeheartedly *while simultaneously realizing* that the commitment rests on a risk of some sort. Knowledge of the religious claim concerned is therefore required to dispel any kind of uncertainty surrounding it. Unless the person in our example *knows* that God exists, his theistic religious commitment can only be *tentative*.

Essentially, the thought here is that knowledge is required to bridge the gap between a state of uncertainty (psychological or propositional) regarding the truth of religious claims and wholehearted religious commitment. Although I have argued earlier that psychological certainty may well obtain without propositional certainty, let us put this point aside for a moment and suppose that only propositional certainty can bring about psychological certainty. Without knowledge (and therefore propositional certainty), one can only be (we are assuming for the moment) psychologically uncertain. If, then, one does not have knowledge about the truth of the religious claim in question, a religious commitment based on that claim will be based on a risk. This is because one will be uncertain about the truth of the belief that motivates that commitment.

But why, we must now ask, is it not possible to acknowledge the risk involved in believing in the truth of a religious claim while committing oneself wholeheartedly to its truth? Why does one need certainty *of any kind* to have

64   *Classical scholastic fideism in Islam*

wholehearted religious commitment? Those who think that knowledge is required for wholehearted religious commitment appear to be assuming that recognizing risk entails a commitment that is tentative. But this assumption is false because grounds that are not truth-conductive may allow one to have a wholehearted religious commitment. Furthermore, one can sustain such a commitment while also recognizing the risk that the belief underlying and motivating this commitment is false. In some cases, *practical* or *prudential* considerations may factor into one's religious commitment. In Pascal's famous Wager Argument mentioned earlier, the essential idea is that, in a situation of epistemic uncertainty regarding God's existence, it is in one's best *interest* to wager for God than to wager against Him.[78] In a similar vein, Robert Adams argues that, in certain situations when the available evidence does not guarantee the truth of a proposition, "the risk of not disregarding the possibility of error would be greater than the risk of disregarding it."[79] He illustrates this point with the following (secular) example:

> A certain woman has a very great ... interest in her husband's love for her. She rightly judges that the objective evidence available to her renders it 99.9 percent probable that he loves her truly. The intensity of her interest is sufficient to cause her some anxiety over the remaining 1/1,000 chance that he loves her not; for her this chance is not too small to be worth worrying about ... But she (very reasonably) wants to disregard the risk of error, in the sense of not hedging her bets, if he does love her. This desire is at least as strong as her desire not to be deceived if he does not love her. Objective reasoning should therefore suffice to bring her to the conclusion that she ought to disregard the risk of error, since by not disregarding it she would run 999 times as great a risk of frustrating one of these desires.[80]

Adams sees that there are parallels between his argument and the basic line of reasoning behind Pascal's Wager. But there is a difference; "whereas Pascal's argument turns on weighing an infinite *interest* against a finite one, [Adams' argument turns] on weighing a large *chance of success* against a small one."[81]

Practical or prudential considerations such as those given by Pascal and Adams may be available to a person who considers commitment to religious faith. In the example I have earlier of a person who bases his religious commitment on evidence that renders it probable to some degree that there is a God, these considerations may be part of his overall reflection regarding his commitment. If the evidence renders the probability of God's existence about one half (or slightly higher), he may commit himself wholeheartedly based on Pascalian considerations related to self-interest. Or, if the evidence makes it very probable though not certain that God exists, his religious commitment may be wholehearted because he judges the likelihood of his being right in thinking that there is a God to be much greater than the small risk of being in error (awareness of the smaller risk may eventually dissipate from his thinking).

Classical scholastic fideism in Islam   65

(c) The nature of philosophical reflection: Thus far, we have seen that al-Ghazali fails to provide good reasons for thinking that Islamic commitment requires knowledge about Islamic claims. I will now say something about his understanding of the nature of philosophical reflection, after which it should become clear how his argument against the viability of a philosophical investigation of Islam fails.

In his discussion of the philosophers in the *Deliverance* as well as in the *Incoherence*, al-Ghazali's chief complaint is that the heretical claims they entertain are unable to be supported by apodictic demonstration, using criteria set up by the philosophers themselves. But then, from this criticism, he concludes that philosophical speculation was unable to satisfy his quest for truth concerning religious matters.[82] But here, one may reasonably object that the nature of philosophical reflection is not exhausted by *deductive* reasoning of the sort seen in apodictic demonstrations. Indeed, most philosophical reflection (and rational reflection in general) is based on *inductive* inferences, which are intended to make the conclusions arrived at probable without necessarily guaranteeing their truth. Many of the typical beliefs we hold, for example, that a friend is reliable, that the campus library is closed at midnight or that taking two pills of aspirin will alleviate a headache, are based on inductive reasoning. Philosophers have applied such reasoning to various philosophical beliefs. To cite a relevant example, Richard Swinburne, perhaps the most prominent contemporary defender of philosophical theism, argues that, while there are no demonstrative proofs for the existence of God, a case based on inductive argumentation shows that "theism is more probable than not."[83]

Nor is it true that philosophical reflection is simply about making sure that we possess knowledge. It is correct to say, as A. J. Ayer does, that philosophers "make statements which are intended to be true, and they commonly rely on argument both to support their own theories and to refute the theories of others."[84] But it does not follow from this that philosophers are interested in securing their claims only on knowledge. Of course, knowledge may be the *ideal*, but philosophers are typically content with just justified beliefs. Indeed, there have been several episodes in the history of philosophy where philosophers have argued that we *cannot* have knowledge about many matters, including religious ones.

It should now be clear just how al-Ghazali's argument against philosophizing about Islamic belief fails. In essence, the argument is that only 'sure and certain' knowledge will do in discussions about religious matters. But, says al-Ghazali, philosophy is unable to provide such knowledge about Islamic belief. Philosophy is, therefore, of no use in alleviating concerns about the truth or rationality of Islamic belief. This argument can be criticized in two ways, as I have shown. First, one can reasonably reject al-Ghazali's view that one must seek *knowledge* about religious matters. Second, one can point out that the discipline of philosophy, understood and appreciated properly, allows for justification that shows how certain beliefs may be rationally held, even if they do not constitute knowledge.

66 *Classical scholastic fideism in Islam*

In examining al-Ghazali's case against applying philosophical methodology to Islamic belief, enough has been said, I think, to show that this case does not succeed. Still, I think it is worth considering just how deeply problematic al-Ghazali's own epistemological approach to religious matters is. One may reasonably or rationally believe something to be the case without *knowing* that it is so. This is what virtually all contemporary philosophers do in entertaining and discussing the plausibility of their views based on reason and argument. But suppose that we are not satisfied with this. Suppose that we want the sort of 'sure and certain' knowledge al-Ghazali demands. Just how far can we get? Not very far, as I will now argue.

(d) Al-Ghazali's epistemological approach examined: Al-Ghazali's epistemological approach in his quest for truth is untenable for the reasons I have already given. Another way of showing its implausibility is to take it seriously and see just how far it can take us. Recall al-Ghazali's criteria for sure and certain knowledge that he provides in the early part of the *Deliverance*:

> S has 'sure and certain knowledge' that p if and only if:
>
> 1 p is manifestly true to S such that S has no doubt about p.
> 2   There is no possibility that S is in error or is deceived about it being the case that p.
> 3   It is inconceivable for S that S is in error or deception about p.
> 4 S has no doubt about p's indefeasibility.

There are a variety of problems in taking these criteria seriously.

(i) One problem with al-Ghazali's criteria for knowledge is that they appear to be self-referentially problematic. Al-Ghazali, as we have seen, insists that all propositions we entertain must pass his criteria for knowledge. But then it seems that this proposal *itself* must be subjected to his criteria. Let's call al-Ghazali's criteria for knowledge K. Do we *know* that K is true based on al-Ghazali's criteria for knowledge? It would appear not. Personally speaking, I do not find K's truth to be manifestly true or without doubt. I think there is good reason to think that I am mistaken if I believe that K is true and I can also conceive of how this can be the case. Moreover, I am open to the possibility that K's (alleged) truth can be defeated. I am reasonably confident that many other people would express similar skepticism towards K.

(ii) Here is a second problem to consider. If we take K seriously, it seems that we cannot know *anything* (except perhaps the fact that we do not know anything). If we can *conceive* the possibility of being in error about the truth of a proposition, then we cannot, according to al-Ghazali, know it. This, however, seems to go against our deeply held commonsense intuitions about what we regard as paradigmatic cases of knowledge. Virtually everyone thinks that they know, for instance, about the antiquity of the world. Now, it is *conceivable* that the world only began very recently, perhaps only a few minutes ago. As Bertrand Russell explains,

Classical scholastic fideism in Islam   67

There is no logical impossibility in the hypothesis that the world sprang into being five minutes ago, exactly as it then was, with a population that "remembered" a wholly unreal past. There is no logically necessary connection between events at different times; therefore nothing that is happening now or will happen in the future can disprove the hypothesis that the world began five minutes ago.[85]

But few would think that merely *conceiving* of this possibility is sufficient to show that we do not know about the antiquity of the world. Now, al-Ghazali does offer a number of skeptical arguments, based on his conceivability requirement, to show that what we regard as paradigmatic cases of knowledge do not, in fact, qualify as such. But most ordinary people would not consider the mere *possibility* of being in error about *p* as a sufficient condition for thinking that one does not know *p*. To be sure, this does not mean that the commonsense view is correct by default, but simply that there is no reason to think it is not. There is a burden of proof issue here. Since al-Ghazali's view about knowledge is a radical one that goes against the view of the *status quo*, the burden of proof rests with him or a defender of his position to make a rationally persuasive case in favor of it. As they stand, al-Ghazali's requirements for a belief to qualify as knowledge appear to be too stringent.

(iii) To further show just how problematic al-Ghazali's criteria for knowledge are, we may add a third reason that focuses on his account of how he was delivered from a situation of extreme skepticism. In the *Deliverance*, after having given us his account of what constitutes knowledge, he tells us he learned that *none* of his beliefs, even those based on sense-data and the self-evident truths of reason, passed his criteria. This resulted in radical skepticism, which could not be refuted by any rational proof since the proof itself would rely on primary cognitions which were being doubted. Recall al-Ghazali's account of his deliverance from radical skepticism after which he trusted in his beliefs based on the self-evident truths of reason and sense-data. The deliverance, he says (to quote a passage cited earlier),

> ... was not achieved by constructing a proof or putting together an argument. On the contrary, it was the effect of a light which God Most High cast into my breast. And that light is the key to most knowledge. Therefore, whoever thinks that the unveiling of truth depends on precisely formulated proofs has indeed straitened the broad mercy of God.

But why think that any of this is true, since al-Ghazali offers no further explanation or argument about his deliverance? According to McCarthy, the 'light' that al-Ghazali refers to is "the 'light' of intellect or intelligence while not excluding some indefinable sort of 'gust of grace'."[86] But, by his own epistemological standards of trusting one's beliefs, one can ask al-Ghazali why this experience of receiving light should be trusted. Using al-Ghazali's own criteria for trusting beliefs, one can argue it is *conceivable* that purported

68 Classical scholastic fideism in Islam

experiences of Divine Grace are mistaken. Perhaps one is deluded, or is engaging in wishful thinking, or is nothing more than a brain in a vat or is being tricked by Descartes' Evil Genius.[87] Al-Ghazali provides no response to such an obvious objection to his account of deliverance from skepticism.

It may be argued in al-Ghazali's defense that his solution to the problem of radical skepticism is *fideist*, so that one shouldn't expect the solution to be based on rational argument. Without any further explanation or argument, however, such a move is arbitrary, especially since al-Ghazali avers that anything short of sure and certain knowledge is unsatisfactory when it comes to any other beliefs. To demand that all other beliefs satisfy the criteria for sure and certain knowledge except for the particular belief that there is a God (who is willing to deliver people from skepticism) is just special pleading.

(iv) Here is one final, theological argument against adopting al-Ghazali's criteria for knowledge. One of the requirements of al-Ghazali's criteria for knowledge is that our beliefs must be *infallibly justified* in order for them to constitute knowledge. But, given our cognitive limitations as *finite* and *fallible* human creatures, such a demand seems unreasonable. It is unreasonable not only because of our finitude but also because it appears to elevate the powers of human cognition to the same level as those of the Divine Mind. Such a move seems theologically unacceptable. Indeed, al-Ghazali himself, in his work *The Ninety-Nine Beautiful Names of God (al-Maqsad al-asna fi sharh asma' Allah al-husna)*, recognizes several important differences between Divine and human cognition, when he discusses one of the Names of God – *Al-'Alim* (The Omniscient).[88] God's knowledge, he writes, is "the most perfect possible, with respect to its clarity and its disclosure, in such a way that no more evident disclosure or vision can be conceived."[89] But, he says, "man's disclosure, while clear, does not reach the goal beyond which no goal is possible; rather his seeing of things is like seeing them behind a thin veil."[90] Given this disparity between Divine and human cognition, it seems much more reasonable to adopt fallibilism instead of infallibilism in matters of epistemic justification.

4.2 Reply to Al-Ghazali's arguments in favor of Sufism and prophecy

Al-Ghazali's arguments in favor of Sufism and prophecy fail, just like his arguments against philosophizing about Islamic belief. Central to his discussion of the topics of Sufism and prophecy in the *Deliverance* is the concept of *dhawq*, or 'fruitional experience'. According to al-Ghazali, God discloses various truths, some of which may be religious, through fruitional experience. This sort of experience, he maintains, is an aspect of prophecy.

One obvious question that arises in reading al-Ghazali's account of *dhawq* and prophecy is whether the sort of 'prophetic cognition' that he discusses is a bona fide phenomenon. Initially, all that al-Ghazali presents is an *explanation* of how God has created the stage of *nubuwwa* or prophecy beyond the

Classical scholastic fideism in Islam 69

ordinary stages of touch, sight, hearing, taste, discernment and the intellect, through which we can perceive 'supra-rational' truths. But what *argument* is there to suppose that this is true? After giving us an account of prophecy, al-Ghazali does proceed to present a brief argument in this passage, which we saw earlier:

> ... [J]ust as one able only to discern, if presented with things perceptible to the intellect, would reject them and consider them as outlandish, so some men endowed with intellect have rejected the things perceptible to the prophetic power and considered them wildly improbable. That is the very essence of ignorance! For such a man has no supporting reason except that it is a stage he himself has not attained and for him it does not exist: so he supposes that it does not exist in itself.

Here, al-Ghazali seems to be saying that critics and skeptics of the prophetic phenomenon have "no supporting reason" for their reservations except an argument from ignorance: the prophetic phenomenon does not exist because they have not personally experienced it. But, of course, critics and skeptics need not be seen as arguing in this manner. Contrary to what al-Ghazali suggests, they may make the more modest (epistemological) claim that there is no good reason to accept the reality of prophecy (allowing for the possibility that it is true). Furthermore, it is false that there is "no supporting reason" to be skeptical about prophecy.

To show how one can be reasonably skeptical about al-Ghazali's views regarding prophecy, let's focus on his 'parity argument' that appears in the quote above. Here is what this argument essentially says. We would see the mistake made by a person who, while only able to discern, dismisses those things that are only perceptible to the intellect. Similarly, we should regard as mistaken those people who, not having progressed beyond the stage of the intellect, dismiss those things that are only perceptible to prophetic power. This argument is problematic because it rests on a weak analogy. Consider two significant disanalogies. First, the reason that we are quick in regarding as mistaken the person who rejects things perceptible only to the intellect, while not having progressed beyond the stage of discernment, is because *we know that the stage of the intellect exists.* Or, at the very least, we can say that there is a high level of intersubjective agreement among people that the stage of the intellect is something that we all (or most of us) eventually go through in growing up. The same cannot be said about prophecy. It does not seem to be an item of common knowledge that prophecy is a stage that we all eventually go through. This is the first disanalogy in the argument. Second, it seems that what we regard as genuine stages of cognition, such as sight, or hearing, or the intellect, are stages in which we are able to discriminate, with a reasonable degree of confidence, between the proper and improper functioning of the relevant faculties of cognition. We can distinguish between good vision and corneal astigmatism, for instance. We are able to

70 *Classical scholastic fideism in Islam*

discriminate between hearing well, having a noticeable hearing impairment and being completely deaf. But when it comes to prophecy, what are the standards by which we can tell whether someone is genuinely cognizant of prophetic truths or whether he is deluded? Attempting to answer this question reveals a second disanalogy between ordinary states of cognition, such as seeing or hearing, and prophecy.

Now, al-Ghazali appears to be aware of this sort of response that says prophecy is something we don't have any real experience of. A preliminary reply he gives to this objection is that we have an analogical segment of prophecy in our sleep, "[f]or the sleeper perceives the unknown that will take place, either plainly, or in the guise of an image the meaning of which is disclosed by interpretation" (p. 97). Here, al-Ghazali is referring more precisely to the phenomenon of dreaming. In dreams, according to him, we sometimes become aware of the unknown that will occur in the future. Unfortunately, al-Ghazali provides no further evidence or argument for thinking that our dreams sometimes have this prophetic aspect to them. People generally accept that the content of dreams is fictional. Indeed, al-Ghazali himself, in the earlier part of his *Deliverance*, notes that when we wake up from dreams we realize that "all [our] imaginings and beliefs were groundless and unsubstantial." And, as Thomas Hobbes notes, "Someone who says that God has spoken to him in a dream has said no more than he dreamt that God spoke to him."[91] A more direct piece of evidence exists for prophecy, however, in al-Ghazali's opinion. This is knowledge that could not conceivably be obtained through the intellect alone, in particular knowledge of medicine and astronomy. And if we examine this knowledge carefully, we will see that it could only come about through divine inspiration (p. 98). This is a strange argument, as McCarthy notes.[92] Al-Ghazali does not elaborate on what sort of medical and astronomical knowledge this might be nor does he consider the possibility that his reasoning here may be rejected as relying on an argument from incredulity. Even if there were cases of medical and astronomical knowledge the origin of which we could not account for by appealing to ordinary human reason, why think that such knowledge came about through divine inspiration?

5. Some concluding remarks about classical scholastic fideism in Islam

A case against the feasibility of philosophically investigating Islam may be derived from the works of al-Ghazali, as shown in this chapter. Specifically, there are a number of arguments that al-Ghazali presents in his autobiography *The Deliverance from Error* that may be used to resist philosophical approaches in evaluating the Islamic faith. These arguments are critical of the rational approach seen in *kalam* and *falsifah* and go on to defend a Sufi epistemology based on the reality of prophecy. As I have argued,

Classical scholastic fideism in Islam 71

however, none of these arguments succeed. If there are any objections to be had against conducting a philosophical investigation of Islam, they will not be found in the perspective and approach offered by al-Ghazali, who spearheads the tradition of scholastic fideism in Islam.

The conclusions arrived at in this chapter are of considerable significance. As noted earlier, the 'Proof of Islam' occupies a very high station in the ranks of Muslim thinkers in Islamic history, and his attack on philosophy is regarded by many in the Muslim community as famously successful. As Alam Khundmiri writes,

> [Al-Ghazali] is the acknowledged leader of orthodox Islam. It was he who gave a final and decisive blow to Islamic scholastic philosophy based on Aristotelian and Neoplatonic sources. This was such a decisive blow that philosophy ceased to remain a respectable term in the Islamic world and even powerful counter arguments by Ibn Rushd were not able to revive the respectability once attached to philosophy.[93]

A careful examination of al-Ghazali's criticisms of philosophy reveals that it is not at all as strong as people might think. Indeed, it is high time for those Muslims who think that al-Ghazali had 'refuted philosophy' to reconsider their views about the place of philosophical inquiry into matters of faith.

Thus, far in our survey of potential objections to a philosophical investigation of Islam, we have looked at classical traditionalist and scholastic fideism. In the next chapter, I will look at some anti-rationalistic fideistic arguments found in the works of some contemporary Muslim thinkers.

Notes

1 George Makdisi, 'Ash'arī and The Ash'arites in Islamic Religious History', *Studia Islamica*, 17, (1962), p. 39.
2 Al-Ghazali, *The Incoherence of the Philosophers*, trans. Michael E. Marmura, (Provo: Brigham Young University Press, 1997), p. xv.
3 W. Montgomery Watt, *The Faith and Practice of Al-Ghazālī*, (London: George Allen and Unwin, 1953), p. 14.
4 Kojiro Nakamura, *Ghazali and Prayer*, (Kuala Lumpur: Islamic Book Trust, 2001), p. 3.
5 R. M. Frank, *Al-Ghazālī and The Ash'arite School*, (Durham: Duke University Press, 1994), pp. x; 3.
6 Ibn Rushd, *Decisive Treatise*, p. 22.
7 For those who are interested in contemporary debates about how to understand and interpret al-Ghazali's views on theology and philosophy, perhaps the best place to begin is Frank Griffel's work *Al-Ghazālī's Philosophical Theology*, (Oxford: Oxford University Press, 2009).
8 See, for example, Michael E. Marmura's brief biographical article on al-Ghazālī, 'Al-Ghazālī', in Peter Adamson and Richard C. Taylor (eds.), *The Cambridge Companion to Arabic Philosophy*, (Cambridge: Cambridge University Press, 2005), pp. 137–154.

72 *Classical scholastic fideism in Islam*

9 Al-Ghazali himself states that the *Incoherence* is a work of *kalam*. See Chapter 2, p. 47.
10 Al-Ghazali, *The Incoherence of the Philosophers*, pp. 1–2.
11 Ibid., p. 2.
12 Ibid.
13 Ibid.
14 Ibid., pp. 2–3.
15 Ibid., p. 3.
16 Ibid.
17 Ibid.
18 Ibid.
19 Ibid.
20 Ibid., pp. 6–7.
21 See ibid., p. 8ff. This point appears again in al-Ghazali's work *The Deliverance from Error*, discussed later in this chapter.
22 Ibid., p. 9.
23 See Chapter 3.
24 Al-Ghazali, *Incoherence*, p. xxi.
25 Ibid., p. 230.
26 Ibid.
27 Ibid.
28 Ibid., p. 46. Italics mine.
29 Marmura, 'Al-Ghazali', p. 141.
30 Dennis Morgan Davis Jr., *Al-Ghazālī on Divine Essence: A Translation from the Iqtisād Fī Al-I'tiqad with Notes and Commentary*, (PhD thesis submitted to the University of Utah, 2005), p. 72.
31 Ibid., p. 73.
32 Ibid.
33 Ibid.
34 Ibid.
35 Ibid.
36 Ibid., p. 79.
37 Ibid., pp. 80–82.
38 Ibid., p. 88.
39 Ibid., p. 92.
40 Ibid., pp. 92–94.
41 Ibid., pp. 94–95.
42 Ibid., pp. 95–96.
43 Ibid., pp. 96–97.
44 This has been translated into English and titled *Freedom and Fulfillment*, by Richard McCarthy, (Boston: Twayne Publishers, 1980).
45 Ibid., p. 69.
46 Ibid., p. 81.
47 Ibid., p. 89ff.
48 Watt, *op. cit.*, pp. 11–12.
49 Unless otherwise stated, all subsequent references to page numbers will be to McCarthy's translation of this work.
50 McCarthy, *Freedom and Fulfillment*, p. 115, note 3.
51 One might wonder whether condition (4) is different from (1). It seems to me that it is, because condition (4) introduces a reference to (future) indefeasibility that is not present in (1). This reference is, however, present in condition (2). Condition (4) states that S has no doubt about condition (2).
52 Talk of 'internal' and 'external' justification-conferring conditions (in order for a belief to be justified, or constitute knowledge) features prominently in

Classical scholastic fideism in Islam 73

contemporary discussions in epistemology. See, for example, Hilary Kornblith, *Epistemology: Internalism and Externalism*, (Cambridge: MIT Press, 2001).

53 Muhammad Ali Khalidi, *Medieval Islamic Philosophical Writings*, (Cambridge: Cambridge University Press, 2005), p. xxvi.

54 The reason why his resolution is labeled as 'fideist' by Khalidi is because al-Ghazali simply asserts (taking 'on faith') that God delivered him from his crisis of extreme skepticism. Khalidi elaborates, contrasting al-Ghazali's attempt to solve the problem of skepticism with that of Descartes:

> The parallels with Descartes' intellectual crisis and bout of scepticism, as recounted in the Discourse on Method and the Meditations on First Philosophy, have often been noted. However, the similarity between the two accounts stops more or less at the point at which the two philosophers find themselves in a state of radical doubt. After that, Ghazālī's solution may be regarded as fideist, while Descartes' is plainly rationalist. Unlike Descartes, Ghazālī makes no attempt to prove the existence of God ... Indeed he advances a reason as to why there can be no rational escape route from a situation of extreme skepticism, pointing out that a proof can only be given by employing certain first principles, but if these are not accepted by the skeptic, then no proof is forthcoming. That is why the fideist solution is the only one open to him, and why he relies on a light from God to restore some of his basic beliefs.
>
> (Ibid)

55 The Batinites were a group of people belonging to an esoteric Ismaili sect among the Shi'ite community during al-Ghazali's time. One of their distinctive and prominent doctrines is the view that religious knowledge can be obtained only from the teachings of an infallible Imam.

56 Khalidi, *op. cit.*, p. xxv.

57 See discussions seventeen to twenty in this work.

58 Stephen Menn, 'The Discourse on the Method and the Tradition of Intellectual Autobiography', in Jon Miller and Brad Inwood (eds.), *Hellenistic and Early Modern Philosophy*, (Cambridge: Cambridge University Press, 2003), pp. 166–167. Italics mine.

59 See Kant's *Critique of Pure Reason*, trans. Norman Kemp Smith, (New York: Macmillan, 1929).

60 The 'exchanging of moral qualities', as McCarthy explains, "refers to a moral change, i.e. the acquiring of virtues," p. 133, note 164.

61 McCarthy, p. 133, note 162. McCarthy elaborates on his choice of the English phrase thus: "*dhawq* is not simply a kind of cognition, but an immediate experience accompanied by savoring, or relishing, and enjoyment, i.e. what I like to call a fruitional (fruitive) experience," ibid.

62 The philosophical concept of *dhawq* was not restricted to al-Ghazali's discussion of it, or even, for that matter, to discussions among Muslim thinkers of his time. For instance, this concept plays a central role in the model of Jewish religious epistemology crafted by the famous thinker, and critic of philosophical theism, Judah Ha-Levi (d. 1141). In his well-known work, the *Kuzari*, one of the central claims, as Diana Lobel writes, is that "direct religious experience and not logical demonstration stands at the heart of Judaism," Diana Lobel, *Between Mysticism and Philosophy: Sufi Language of Religious Experience in Judah Ha-Levi's Kuzari*, (Albany: SUNY Press, 2000), p. 89. Consider, as an example, the following epiphany in the *Kuzari* involving the Pagan King of the Khazars and the *Haver* (interlocutor):

> *The King:* Now it has become clear to me the difference between God and Lord, and I understand what [the difference is] between the God of Abraham and the God of Aristotle. The Lord, may He be blessed, one longs for with a

74 *Classical scholastic fideism in Islam*

longing of taste [*dhawq*] and witness [*mushāhada*], while we [only] incline logically [*qiyāsan*] to God.

And this tasting prompts one who has attained it to be consumed in love for him, and to [prefer] death to being without him; while that logic [*qiyās*] [only] shows that veneration is incumbent as long as one does not suffer or bear hardship on account of it ...

The Haver: Whereas Abraham bore justly [all that] he suffered in Ur of the Chaldeans, in emigration, in circumcision, in the removal of Ishmael, and in the distressing resolution to sacrifice Isaac – for he perceived [*shahāda*] the *'amr ilāhī* by taste, not by logic; as quoted by Lobel, pp. 89–90.

63 The example of drunkenness does not really help to bring this out clearly, since, as al-Ghazali himself points out, the drunken man (typically) has no knowledge by awareness of his drunkenness!

64 Ibid., note 200.

65 *Ab esse ad posse valet consequentia* ("From the fact that something exists, it follows that it is possible"). This is a medieval rule of inference, one that can also be found in Aristotle.

66 This is not an easy task, given that al-Ghazali's writings reveal an intellectual position that is, at best, simply varied and, at worst, incoherent. Several authors have struggled with the difficulty of trying to make sense of al-Ghazali's intellectual position as a whole. Perhaps this problem is understandable, even if irresolvable, if one takes it to be a reflection of al-Ghazali's turbulent life. As Ebrahim Moosa writes:

> [Al-Ghazali's] portrait is multifaceted. He was a person committed to many political and intellectual causes. But his embrace of law, politics, mysticism, and philosophy did not follow a uniform path ... If the unpredictability of life shapes the career of a great person, then it is significant that Ghazālī's life was radically unpredictable and followed no logical pattern.
>
> Ebrahim Moosa, *Ghazālī and The Poetics of Imagination*,
> (Chapel Hill: UNC Press, 2005), pp. 7–8

67 Robert Audi, *Epistemology: A Contemporary Introduction to the Theory of Knowledge*, Second edition, (Abingdon: Routledge, 2003), p. 4.

68 Jane I. Smith, 'Imān and Islām', in Micea Eliade (ed.), *The Encyclopedia of Religion*, (New York: Macmillan, 1987), p. 119.

69 For a comprehensive Islamic discussion of *iman*, see Ibn Taymiyyah's *Book of Faith (Kitab Al-Iman)*, trans. Salman Hassan Al-Ani and Shadia Ahmad Tel, (Kuala Lumpur: Islamic Book Trust, 2009).

70 Audi, *op. cit.*, pp. 224–225.

71 Ibid., p. 224.

72 Ibid.

73 Ibid., p. 225.

74 Pascal's *Pensées*, trans. Honor Levi, (Oxford: Oxford University Press, 1995), p. 155.

75 Ibid., pp. 155–156.

76 William James, *The Will to Believe*, (New York: Dover Publications, 1956), p. 9.

77 Ibid.

78 Pascal, *Pensées*, pp. 152–156.

79 Robert Merrihew Adams, 'Kierkegaard's Arguments against Objective Reasoning in Religion', in *The Virtue of Faith*, (Oxford: Oxford University Press, 1987), p. 28.

80 Ibid., pp. 28–29.

81 Ibid., p. 29. Italics mine.

82 Al-Ghazali, *Deliverance*, pp. 81–82.

Classical scholastic fideism in Islam   75

83 Richard Swinburne, *The Existence of God*, (Oxford: Clarendon Press, 2004), p. 342.
84 A. J. Ayer, *The Problem of Knowledge*, (London: Macmillan, 1956), p. 1.
85 Bertrand Russell, *The Analysis of Mind*, (London: George Allen & Unwin, 1921), pp. 159–160.
86 McCarthy, p. 122, note 44.
87 See the first two meditations in his 'Meditations on First Philosophy', in Elizabeth S. Haldane et al. (eds.), *Descartes: Key Philosophical Writings*, (Hertfordshire: Wordsworth, 1997), p. 138ff.
88 Translated with notes by David B. Burrell and Nazih Dahir, (The Islamic Texts Society, 1995), p. 80.
89 Ibid.
90 Ibid.
91 Thomas Hobbes as cited by Richard E. Creel, *Thinking Philosophically*, (Malden: Blackwell Publishing, 2001), p. 32.
92 "The argument from the knowledge found in medicine and astronomy may seem strange," McCarthy, p. 138, n. 204.
93 Alam Khundmiri, 'Al-Ghazali's Repudiation of Causality', in M.T. Ansari (ed.), *Secularism, Islam and Modernity: Selected Essays of Alam Khundmiri*, (New Delhi: Sage Publications, 2001), p. 120.

4 Contemporary fideism in Islam

1. Contemporary fideist trends in Islamic thought

Thus far in my examination of anti-rationalist fideism in Islam, I have critically assessed and ultimately rejected both classical traditionalist and scholastic fideism. Despite the objections and criticisms that can be leveled against it, however, anti-rationalistic fideism dominates contemporary Islamic thought. Many Muslims today view philosophy with suspicion, if they do not outright reject its operation in the religious domain. Many of the reasons that they cite were addressed in my examination of classical and scholastic fideism in Islam. Several Muslims think that philosophy is simply impermissible and forbidden from a religious point of view. One can find numerous *fatwas* (legal opinions usually issued by scholars of Islamic jurisprudence) attesting to this.[1] Other Muslims who might be sympathetic to the permissibility of philosophizing about Islamic belief nevertheless maintain that it is of little use in the religious domain since it cannot provide any definite answers to ultimate questions about God, humanity, the universe, etc. For instance, in one of his public lectures, the popular Islamic preacher, Yasir Qadhi, describes philosophy as a "science whose basic premise is flawed."[2] This basic premise, he explains, is that "via man's intellect, the ultimate truths of life can be arrived at."[3] He then proceeds to dismiss philosophy on the grounds that only Divine Revelation can provide us with the ultimate truths about life.[4]

As an example of a contemporary authoritative ruling that makes claims about both the impermissibility and limitations of philosophy, we can consider the edict found in the juridical compendium based on the Shafi'ite school of thought, authored by Ahmad ibn Naqib al-Misri (d. 1386), titled *The Reliance of the Traveller* (*'Umdat al-salik*). Although originally written several centuries ago, the work was recently translated into English by the American Muslim scholar Nuh Ha Mim Keller[5] and received official certification from al-Azhar, one of the world's foremost institutions of Islamic learning.[6] In their certification, al-Azhar notes that the work "conforms to the practice and faith of the orthodox Sunni Community."[7] In the first book of the compendium, which discusses Sacred Knowledge, we find that philosophy is listed along with sorcery, magic and astrology as 'forbidden knowledge'.[8] What orthodoxy finds objectionable about philosophy, as Kellar notes, are its

Contemporary fideism in Islam 77

... cosmological theories and all-too-human attempts to solve ultimate questions about man, God, life after death, and so forth, without the divinely revealed guidance of the Koran or sunna: Any opinion that contradicts a well-known tenet of Islamic belief that there is scholarly consensus upon ... is unbelief (kufr), and is unlawful to learn or teach, except by way of explaining that it is unlawful.[9]

Here, then, we have a sanctioned denunciation of philosophy based on the alleged impermissibility of its practice and its limitations in providing answers to ultimate questions about human existence and destiny.

In this chapter, I will continue my discussion of Islamic anti-rationalistic fideism by looking at its contemporary defenders. Doing this will allow us to see how fideistic thought has developed in Islamic history and whether its evolution has resulted in a more plausible or defensible position. Although anti-rationalistic fideism is predominant among Muslims to-day, it is difficult to find a contemporary Islamic thinker who provides a systematic defense of it. As far as I am aware, there are no obvious Islamic parallels of Christian fideists, such as Soren Kierkegaard (d. 1855) or Karl Barth (d. 1968), in the more recent part of Islamic tradition. Nevertheless, one can easily construct systematic arguments for anti-rationalistic fid-eism by examining the works of several contemporary Muslim thinkers. In what follows, I shall present and evaluate some of these arguments by looking at the writings of two well-known Muslim thinkers of the 20th century, Sayyid Abu A'la Maududi (d. 1979) and Sayyid Qutb (d. 1966). Maududi and Qutb are primarily recognized as the principal figures of 'Islamism' and Islamic fundamentalism; both advocated a radical view that it is every Muslim's duty to work towards establishing Islam as a global political entity. Although the subject of politics forms a major topic in their writings, one soon discovers that anti-rationalistic fideism pervades their works and influences much of their thinking about reli-gious matters.

2. Maududi's fideism

2.1 *Maududi on the 'Fallacy of Rationalism'*

In several of Maududi's writings, one can find threads of reasoning that are sympathetic towards, if not completely accepting of, anti-rationalistic fide-ism. The core of Maududi's Islamic thought is nicely summarized as follows by Malise Ruthven:

[Maududi's] basic premise is that Islam is entirely self-sufficient and does not need to explain itself in terms other than its own. He is not interested in harmonizing his Islamic ideology with other systems. For Maududi, Islam is perfect and needs no justification.[10]

78 *Contemporary fideism in Islam*

An example of Maududi's fideistic thinking can be seen in a paper that he published in the early 1930s called 'Fallacy of Rationalism'.[11] My assessment of Maududi's fideism will be based on a number of arguments that he presents in this paper.[12]

Maududi begins his critical piece on rationalism by quoting at length from an article written by an unnamed Muslim graduate who provides an account of his (the graduate's) tour of China and Japan (pp. 207–208). He provides several quotes where the graduate questions various Islamic injunctions and doctrines. The graduate asks, for instance, whether the Islamic ruling that prohibits the consumption of pork is universal, since he wants to adopt a lenient attitude towards those Chinese converts to Islam who adore eating pork (ibid). He also questions the reasonableness of the traditional Islamic view that non-Muslims, which would include the majority of the Chinese population, are destined for Hell; it is unreasonable to maintain that such happy and prosperous people, who lead a calm and quiet life, would deserve Hell (ibid). The essence of real religion, according to Maududi's quoted author, is fair dealing and doing good deeds, and its purpose is to convince us that we are accountable for our doings, either in this life or in the one to come. Demanding more than this, as in the specific requirements that one finds in Shariah Law, will only stifle the progress of the Muslim nation (ibid).

In response, Maududi says that the article in which these views are found is "a self-explanatory example of the mind and thinking of our new generation [of Muslims] with modern education" (ibid). Although the new Muslim generation grew up in a Muslim society and has strong ties to it, it has become very deeply influenced by Western thought and rationalism (pp. 208–209). But the pretension to rationalism, avers Maududi, is just that and no more:

> Whenever these gentlemen speak on religious issues they are mostly irrelevant and do not even know what they are talking about. Neither are their premises correct, nor do they argue in any logical sequence or try to draw correct conclusions, so much so that they can not [*sic*] even determine their own standpoint while arguing ... Loose-thinking is the glaring feature of their commentaries on religion.
>
> (p. 209)

What, then, is the problem in trying to apply rationalist thought to Islamic belief and practice? Bringing the discussion back to the article that he quoted from earlier, Maududi notes that "the article does not indicate whether the writer is speaking as a Muslim or a non-Muslim" (p. 210). But why does this matter?

Maududi answers as follows, providing an initial argument against rationalist tendencies within an Islamic context:

> Speaking on Islam, one is either a Muslim or a non-Muslim. If he speaks as a Muslim, may he be orthodox, a liberal thinker, or a reformer,

Contemporary fideism in Islam 79

whatever be the case, he is expected to talk within the orbit of Islam with the Quran as the final authority and within the fundamentals of religion and the laws of Shari'ah as enunciated in the holy Quran. Whoever does not believe in the holy Quran as the final authority, and considers its injunctions as open to discussion, automatically goes out of the pale of Islam and thus loses every right to speak as a Muslim. If one speaks as a non-Muslim, he will have every right to criticize the principles and injunctions enunciated by the Quran in whatever manner he likes, because he does not believe in the holy Quran as the final word of Allah. But, speaking as a non-Muslim, he will have no right to pose himself as a Muslim and try to explain to the Muslims the meanings of Islam and the ways and means to promote Islam. Any sensible person talking about Islam with sense and reason will have to decide whether he is going to speak as a Muslim or a non-Muslim and, while giving his opinion, will fully observe the logical requirements of the position he has chosen.

But it is against all cannons [*sic*] of justice and reason to call oneself a Muslim, [... assume] the right to criticize the principles and laws given by the Quran, question the Quran's authority, and yet try to advise and guide Muslims. It is nothing but an attempt to use antonyms as synonyms. Paradoxically, it means that a person can be a Muslim as well as a non-Muslim at the same time and remain within the pale of Islam and outside its fold simultaneously.

(p. 210)

The argument contained in this extended passage essentially maintains that one cannot simultaneously maintain the role of a Muslim believer and a rationalist. If one is a Muslim, one cannot, for instance, question Qur'anic injunctions from an external or 'outsider' perspective. Conversely, a person who does question these injunctions from such a perspective cannot be a Muslim. Here is another way of looking at this: Maududi is arguing that, as a Muslim, one cannot step 'outside' the framework of the Islamic religion to critically consider the reasonableness of Islamic belief and practice. This reason for this, he explains, is that it would mean that one does not consider the Qur'an to be the 'final authority' in religious matters. Doing this results in one leaving the pale of Islam.

Maududi presents another similar kind of argument in the following passage:

Rationally, there can be only two positions of a person with relevance to Islam. Either he is a Muslim or a non-Muslim. If he is a Muslim, it means that he has conceded that Allah is the Supreme Authority and the holy Prophet is the authentic Messenger of Allah. He has also committed that he will surrender unconditionally to all the injunctions conveyed

80 Contemporary fideism in Islam

to him by the authentic Messenger of Allah. He has thus surrendered his right to demand any rational proof or argument for each and every injunction.

(p. 217)

In this argument, Maududi thinks that being a Muslim believer means that one has conceded certain things. Specifically, one has conceded that Allah is the Supreme Authority and the Prophet of Islam is His Messenger. In doing so, one has surrendered unconditionally to all of the religious injunctions conveyed to us by the Prophet. Such unconditional surrender includes surrendering the right to demand proof or argument about Islamic belief and practice.[13]

A third argument is given by Maududi that draws an analogy between secular and religious systems:

No government can stay even for a moment if every person starts demanding rational justification for its orders and refuses to submit to any order without getting its satisfactory justification. No army can be called an army if every soldier starts seeking the reason for his commander's orders and demanding his satisfaction before compliance. No school, no college, no association, in short no system can work on the basis of satisfying each and every individual prior to the compliance of its order.

(p. 217)

In explaining this argument, Maududi points out that anyone who joins a system or organization does so only on the condition that he or she will believe in the authority of that system as the supreme authority and obey its injunctions. Subjecting obedience to personal satisfaction leads to revolt (ibid). No government would accept an attitude of revolt against what is established law and would try the culprit for rebellion. In the case of the army, the person would be court martialed. In an educational institution, he or she would be immediately expelled. And, says Maududi, inferring his intended conclusion after citing what he takes to be appropriate analogues, in the case of religion such a person would be declared an apostate (pp. 217–218).

2.2 Reply to Maududi's arguments against rationalism

There are at least two problems with Maududi's first argument against rationalism. A critical premise in this argument says that anyone who considers Qur'anic injunctions as open to discussion fails to accept as the final authority. If by 'open to discussion', Maududi is referring to an allowance for *questioning the commitment* to these injunctions, then his claim here is surely false. There seems to be no incompatibility between accepting the authoritative nature of the Qur'an while also maintaining that Qur'anic injunctions are open to discussion. Indeed, one might argue that accepting the authority of the Qur'an *requires* that its injunctions are open to discussion in at least trying to *understand* what God has revealed in it. The need for interpretive understanding arises because of the Qur'an's historical context. As Kenneth Cragg explains,

> There have long been those who interpreted the Qur'ān's authority and status as somehow absolving it from historical conditions, who have even cited its traditional non-chronological arrangement in their support. As the eternal and final revelation the Scripture is, no doubt, in history. But once in, by divine decree, it disengages from mere time and possesses a kind of absolutely, historically unconditioned, quality which makes a sense of its context superfluous.
>
> Such assumptions, of course, jeopardize–indeed disqualify–the whole possibility of revelation itself ... [T]hey imply an entire misguidedness in the whole instinct of Tradition to draw guidance from the time and place of Muhammad. They also overlook or mistake the role of the context of revelation in its very content and the place of 'the occasions of *tanzīl*', or the points in the story at which *wahy* [revelation] interposed its message. For inspiration was not seldom an actual commentary on a situation or a response to an interrogative latent or articulate in events of the prophetic biography. The Qur'ān could not have been revelatory had it also not been 'eventful'. As itself a total event within events its study, like its quality, must live in history ...
>
> To speak in this context of 'the struggle to mean', does not argue any intentional compromise of the authority of revelation, but rather to see it proceeding within the fabric of the real world...[14]

Arguably, then, the notion that the Qur'an, as a historical revelation, reveals the will of God necessarily requires interpretation in order to understand it properly. Indeed, Islamic theology itself recognizes this point in the concept of an 'occasion of revelation'. Based on this reason alone, Maududi is wrong to argue that one cannot both accept the Qur'an as decisively authoritative and consider its injunctions as open to discussion.

A second problem with Maududi's initial argument against rationalism is his insistence that anyone who does not accept the Qur'an as the *final* authority goes out of the pale of Islam. But this claim is not evidently true. Notice that Maududi's claim here is *not* that anyone who does not consider the Qur'an to be authoritative (in a general sense) goes out of the pale of Islam. Rather, his claim is that anyone who does not consider the Qur'an as the *final* authority goes out of the pale of Islam. So, according to Maududi, it is not enough for a Muslim to believe that the Qur'an is God's Word, that its authority carries great weight, etc. One must *also* believe that the authority

82 *Contemporary fideism in Islam*

of the Qur'an is 'final'. An initial problem in evaluating this claim is that it is not clear what Maududi means by the 'final authority' of the Qur'an. One way to interpret it is to see the Qur'an as the ultimate standard by which all other things are measured. That is to say, one who believes in the Qur'an to be Divine Revelation is also committed to the view that it cannot be subsumed under any other criterion of assessment. Defenders of this claim may point out that the Qur'an refers to itself as *al-furqan* ('the criterion') in a few places (e.g., Qur'an 25:1).

Despite what Maududi says, however, there is no good reason to think that failing to regard belief in the Qur'an as autonomous puts a person out of the pale of Islam. Suppose that a person believes in the authoritativeness of the Qur'an but that this belief is *conditional* on the availability of supporting proofs and arguments (i.e., the person takes the Qur'an to be authoritative *because* she judges this belief to be support by rational considerations). What, one may ask, is so blasphemous or heretical about holding this sort of position? A defender of Maududi may respond here by arguing that such a stance commits one to the view that the 'authority of reason' is superior to the authority of God's revelation. But this is not a persuasive reply. If revelation is judged by reason, this does not mean that the former is 'inferior' to the latter. As Shabbir Akhtar explains,

> Allah is indeed the best of judges. It is of course true – indeed necessarily true – that what God says about us is superior in insight to what we may say about ourselves, our capacities, or about God. To say, however, that God's (alleged) revelation should be assessed by use of the normal methods of scrutiny is not to deny the ultimacy – or primacy (whichever sounds better) – of God's views. It is merely a comment on how to seek to determine what God's views actually are, and the recommendation is that we should use the only apparatus we possess, namely, the methods of reason. (Remember that rejecting the supremacy of *reason* here is one thing; rejecting the importance of *reasoning* is quite another.)[15]

Rational considerations may play an important role in determining (to the best of one's abilities) what God wills and what He requires of us. Such considerations may also provide one with justification for believing that God exists, that God wills certain things, etc. There is no inconsistency in maintaining that there is rational justification to support the belief that God (whose authority is ultimate) exists and has commanded certain things or in maintaining that such belief is conditioned on the availability of such justification.[16]

Here is another noteworthy point. If belief in the authority of the Qur'an was truly autonomous for believing Muslims, there could not in principle be *any* rational considerations that could change their minds about its authority. But this is odd. Suppose several manuscripts predating the Prophet Muhammad by five hundred years are discovered in some

Contemporary fideism in Islam 83

ruins close to Mecca. Suppose also that the content of these manuscripts is identical to what is contained in the Qur'an. Were this to happen and the findings were confirmed beyond any doubt to be genuine, one can imagine how even devout Muslims would be prepared to reconsider their commitments to Islam. If this is correct, it follows that the Muslim belief in the Qur'an as Divine Revelation is based on and sustained by at least basic rational considerations. There does not seem to be anything blasphemous or heretical about this view at all. Indeed, the Qur'an itself explicitly accepts such a point, allowing for a rational assessment of its claims about being a revelation from God. "Do they not consider the Qur'an (with care)?" asks its Author. "Had it been from other than Allah, they would surely have found therein much discrepancy" (Qur'an 4:82).

What, though, of the Qur'an's reference to itself as *al-furqan* ('the criterion')? Might not this label be taken to mean that belief in the Qur'an's authority should be autonomous for committed Muslims? If so, would this not then exempt such belief from rational considerations? While it is true that the Qur'an does refer to itself as 'the criterion', it is not at all clear that such a reference will necessarily exclude rational considerations about religious matters. Certain exegetes of the Qur'an have interpreted its description of itself as *al-furqan* to include rational considerations. The term first appears in Qur'an 2:53: "And [recall] when We gave Moses the Scripture and criterion (*furqan*) that perhaps you would be guided." In commenting on this verse and specifically on the Arabic word *furqan*, Muhammad Asad writes:

> Muhammad 'Abduh amplifies [this] interpretation of *al-furqān* (adopted by Tabarī, Zamakhsharī and other greater commentators) by maintaining that it applies also to "human reason, which enables us to distinguish the true from the false" ... While the term *furqān* is often used in the Qur'ān to describe one or another of the revealed scriptures, and particularly the Qur'ān itself, it has undoubtedly also the connotation pointed out by 'Abduh: for instance, in 8:29, where it clearly refers to the faculty of moral valuation which distinguishes every human being who is truly conscious of God.[17]

Given the Qur'an's constant invitation to reflect and think about creation (e.g., 3:191; 7:185), such an interpretation of *furqan* seems plausible. On this interpretation, appealing to the Qur'an's status as *al-furqan* fails to show that belief in its authority should be autonomous for committed Muslims.

These criticisms of Maududi's first argument against rationalism may also be applied to his second argument, since there are similarities between the two. The crux of Maududi's second argument is that being a Muslim entails that one holds Allah and His Prophet to constitute 'supreme authority', and this, in turn, means that one has surrendered *unconditionally* to all of the injunctions conveyed to us by the Prophet. As I have already argued, there is no incompatibility between seeing God as the final or supreme authority and

84 *Contemporary fideism in Islam*

having this belief conditioned on rational proofs and arguments. But further criticisms can be raised here. Maududi fails to make a distinction between *mere commitment to religious injunctions* and *the sake for which one commits to religious injunctions*. Islamic injunctions, such as prayer and fasting, serve to enrich one's commitment to God. According to mainstream Islamic tradition, this commitment should be based on *taqwa*, or 'God-consciousness'. This concept features prominently in the Islamic faith (see, for instance, Qur'an 59:18). It is for the sake of taqwa that one pursues injunctions such as prayer and fasting (e.g., Qur'an 20:14, 2:183). The *mere* ritualization of injunctions is not enough. If this is correct, then Maududi is wrong to think that a Muslim's commitment to injunctions conveyed to us by the Prophet is unconditional. Moreover, one can see how reasoned reflection or argument can play a role in thinking about whether one is indeed basing one's practice of religious injunctions on *taqwa* (e.g., think about how rational deliberation plays a role when a person wonders whether she is doing the right thing for the wrong reasons).

Maududi's third argument against rationalism is fairly straightforward, making two basic claims. First, Maududi states that no organization, including governments, armies and schools, can function properly if every member of that organization demands rational justification for each and every one of the orders it issues. If a person joins an organization, he or she must conform to the authority of that organization, regarding it as the supreme authority and refraining from seeking rational justification for any injunctions issued. Second, Maududi argues that a person's insisting on such rational justification from within an organization would lead to a revolt and this, he maintains, would be regarded as unacceptable from the point of view of any organization. A person who demands rational justification from within an organization for each of the injunctions it issues would be expelled from it. It follows then that one should not seek rational justification for each and every religious injunction if one is a member of a religious organization. Otherwise, one would be excluded from it and declared an apostate.

This is a very poor argument. It is reminiscent of an argument against *ijtihad* presented by Ibn Qudama that I examined earlier.[18] The basic problem here is that Maududi addresses a straw man. The rationalists he is trying to rebut need not be seen as making the extravagant claim that partaking in *each and every* religious injunction requires rational justification *every time* for *every member* who is part of a religion. A more charitable and plausible interpretation of the rationalists' claim is that, under *certain circumstances*, *certain members* of a religion are within their rights in *sometimes* asking for rational justification for *certain* injunctions. Thus interpreted, this claim seems perfectly reasonable. And, indeed, similar requests that might arise in other organizations appear reasonable too and not as ridiculous as Maududi makes them out to be. In a school, for example, some students may sometimes reasonably ask what good reasons there are for the school to persist with a policy of extended detention if they think that better disciplinary measures are available to curb improper behavior.

There is a significant difference between such a claim and the claim that *all students* within a school have a right to ask for rational justification *every time* for *all* of the injunctions that it issues.

3. Qutb's fideism

3.1 Qutb on Islam as 'the foundation of knowledge': the 'Argument from Divine Sovereignty'

Maududi's writings strongly influenced the Egyptian Islamist Sayyid Qutb, whom Peter R. Demant labels "Islam's most important fundamentalist thinker."[19] Some of the principles that Maududi developed and incorporated into his theological outlook were also adapted by Qutb. One of these principles relevant to our discussion is what Demant calls "anti-apology."[20] According to this principle,

> Islam proves and justifies itself, and hence is in no need of either external validation or harmonization with other ideologies. The Qur'an is true because it says that it is God's word. Because Islam is perfect (having been given by God), it needs no adaptation – only the right application.[21]

Although the principle of anti-apology pervades the writings of both Maududi and Qutb, it is the latter who appeals to it especially in his more explicit and forceful rejection of rationalism and the philosophical sciences. Qutb's concern with keeping these sciences at bay from Islam was present for several years of his life. As Roxanne L. Euben notes,

> [I]t is through the exposition of the nature and opposition of an originally Western rationalist epistemology and the truths of Islamic revelation that Qutb's terms and targets are most carefully delineated. Indeed, despite the radical shifts in his thought over the years, for Qutb the tension between these two approaches to knowledge remains a consistent preoccupation and constant source of anxiety.[22]

Qutb is fully aware that the history of Islamic thought bears witness to a rich rationalist and philosophical tradition. Although rational speculation was first used by the early Muslim community to resolve intra-Islamic controversies and disputes, such speculation eventually lead to the autonomous discipline of (Islamic) philosophy – *falsifa*. This science became independent of theology and its religious roots, and this, for Qutb, was disastrous. Euben elaborates further:

> First, Qutb argues that the emergence of an autonomous subject called "philosophy" reflected the successful penetration of non-Islamic methods and concerns – Greek philosophy in particular – into what Qutb

86 *Contemporary fideism in Islam*

regarded as a pure Islamic conception of life, that is, a conception that in its so-called original form had been defined by clear geographic, cultural, and theological boundaries. Thus, for Qutb, the very emergence of philosophy as an intellectual enterprise, Islamic or otherwise, was already an expression of the corrosion of Islam by foreign cultures.

The second disaster philosophy precipitated in Islam is tied to the first: under the shadow of non-Islamic influences, the very enterprise of "philosophy" expanded the legitimate range of human speculation to encompass questions of existence itself. It opened to human enquiry the "whys" as well as the "hows" of the universe. Put another way, philosophy – Islamic, Greek, or Western – is intrinsically corrosive to Islam because it presumes that the meaning of human existence is a legitimate field of human inquiry rather than a mystery known only to God. This presumption is corrosive in part because it is transgressive: it represents human encroachment on the realm of divine authority. But it is also corrosive because it subjects what are essentially self-evident, divine truths to interpretation through human reason, which is by definition limited and fallible.[23]

Some of these concerns and criticisms regarding the philosophical sciences can be found in Qutb's most famous work, *Milestones (Ma'alim fi'l-Tariq)*. Qutb's articulation and defense of his conception of the Islamic worldview in this work contains an explicit criticism and rejection of the philosophical sciences. As with Maududi, the considerations that Qutb presents can be seen as amounting to a defense of anti-rationalistic fideism and a rejection of philosophizing about Islamic belief. In what follows, I shall confine my examination of Qutb's arguments to the section in *Milestones* in which he discusses Islam as the foundation of knowledge.[24]

Qutb begins his discussion of Islam as providing the foundation of knowledge by referring to the *shahada* or Islamic testimony of faith. Affirming the *shahada*, he explains, entails perfect or absolute servitude to God alone (p. 197). Moreover, it means that the Muslim recognizes sovereignty belongs only to God (ibid). Taking his cue from the concept of Divine Sovereignty, Qutb offers what I shall call *The Argument from Divine Sovereignty*. This argument, if successful, shows that it is not permissible for committed Muslims to engage in philosophical speculation regarding religious (Islamic) matters. Qutb begins his argument by pointing out that committing oneself to the view that God is Sovereign means that one is also committed to following the Divine Law. But this Law, according to him, is all-encompassing with respect to the regulation of human life:

From the point of view of Islamic ideology the meaning of God's sovereignty is not confined to receiving legal orders from God alone and then judgments sought in the light of those commands and delivered accordingly. In Islam the meaning of "Divine Law" itself is not restricted to the sphere of legal orders only, not even to the sphere of fundamental regulations of rulership, its system, and its diverse institutions. This limited and narrow concept of Divine Law does not appropriately explain Islamic law and Islamic ideology. What Islam calls Divine Law, covers the entire scheme God has devised for regulating human life. It includes within its sphere the regulation of thoughts and views, fundamentals of statecraft, principles of ethics and culture, laws of transactions, and regulations of knowledge and the arts. The Divine code of law circumscribes every angle of human thought and opinion. It discusses all the nooks and corners of human life whether it pertains to the human concept about the Supreme Being or the Universe or the transcendental realities, which are beyond the grasp of human comprehension and senses; whether it is the creative sphere of life or that of legislation, whether it is the question of man's reality and his nature or a discussion relating to his very status in the universe.

(p. 198)

Because the Divine Law is an all-encompassing plan that God has devised for the regulation of human life, a Muslim is not permitted to acquire knowledge from any other source about a variety of matters:

A Muslim has not the authority to seek guidance and light from any other source and well-head except the Divine one in any matter that pertains to faith, the general concept of life, rituals, morals and dealings, values and standards, politics, and assembly, principles of economics, or the explanation of human history.

(p. 199)

But, immediately after explaining this prohibition, Qutb informs us:

Of course, a Muslim is allowed to imbibe abstract learnings from all the Muslims and non-Muslims alike, for example, Chemistry, Physics, Biology, Astronomy, Medicine, Industry, Agriculture, Administration (to the extent of technical aspects only), Technology, Arts of warfare (from their technical aspect only), and other like learnings, arts, and technology.

(pp. 199–200)

Here, one might initially be puzzled about why one cannot consult any other source but Divine Law in seeking knowledge about matters pertaining to faith, life, morality, etc., while this restriction is relaxed when it comes to matters related to other areas, such as chemistry and physics. For, one might wonder, doesn't Qutb think that the Divine Law is *all-encompassing*? Qutb's response to this question is that the Divine Law is all-encompassing *relative to the regulation of human life*. The restriction

88 Contemporary fideism in Islam

on consulting sources other than Divine Law applies only if these sources purport to provide answers about matters related to regulating human life. For Muslims, views about the meaning of life or the nature of morality, for example, have a bearing on how to live one's life; they are also views that are provided by the Islamic framework. Therefore, seeking guidance about these views from outside this framework is, according to Qutb, forbidden. By contrast, knowledge about, say, chemistry and physics has no such bearing on the regulation of human life or on religion. Hence, acquiring knowledge about purely secular matters from non-Muslim sources is permissible. These matters, he says,

> ... are not concerned with those principles and regulations and laws and canons that organize the lives of individuals and community. They are also not connected with morals and manners, customs and traditions, and those values and standards that command supremacy in society and project their impressions onto society, hence the Muslim need not fear that by imbibing these learnings he would be vulnerable to any flaw in his faith or he would revert to Jahiliyyah.
>
> (p. 200)[25]

Knowledge about matters that pertain to religious faith, however, should be sought from God alone. A Muslim, avers Qutb,

> ... should be fully cognizant that to imbibe light from the Divine revelation in ... matters [that pertain to faith] is a binding demand of God's servitude of the inevitable consequence of the witness wherein it has been proclaimed that there is no god except God and Muhammad ... is the messenger of God.
>
> (p. 200)

It is permissible to study works produced by non-Muslim sources pertaining to faith – works produced by 'Jahili research' – only to expose the mistakes in them and to aid in converting people to the correct concept of life as given by the Islamic faith (p. 200). When it comes to knowledge about matters related to the regulation of human life, there are only two sources, according to Qutb. The first is Islam and the second is Jahiliyyah. Under the rubric of the latter, Qutb includes the following disciplines:

> Philosophy, interpretation of human history, Psychology (with the exception of those observations and disputed opinions that do not investigate the interpretation and explanation), Ethics, Religions and their comparative study, Social Sciences and Humanities (leaving observations, statistics and directly acquired information, and the fundamental concepts that are developed on their basis).
>
> (p. 201)

Contemporary fideism in Islam 89

Because of the Jahili origins of these sciences, they "are at loggerheads with religion in their fundamental principles, and nurse an explicit or implicit grudge against the concept of religion ordinarily and the Islamic concept particularly" (ibid). As a Muslim, one can acquire knowledge about matters pertaining to the regulation of human life only from within the Islamic worldview. It is impermissible for a Muslim to step outside Islam, into the world of Jahiliyyah, to obtain knowledge about these matters from non-Muslim sources. "A Muslim cannot," writes Qutb, "simultaneously benefit from both these contradictory sources, i.e., the Divine source and the Jahiliyyah" (p. 203).

It should be clear by now how Qutb's Argument from Divine Sovereignty attempts to rule out the permissibility of philosophical speculation about religious (Islamic) matters for committed Muslims. Philosophy, for Qutb, is a discipline that has a bearing on religious matters and on this point he is surely correct. Philosophy includes a significant prescriptive element, aiming to inform us about what we should believe and do. Since Islam purports to do the same thing, however, there is a clash between these two sources. Qutb emphatically declares that he is not just offering his own opinion in arguing that it is impermissible for a Muslim to step outside the parameters of Islam to acquire knowledge about matters pertaining to the regulation of human life. "[T]he matter is too high," he says, "that a decision cannot be taken on the basis of personal opinion" (ibid). No less an Authority than God and His Messenger prescribe this prohibition (pp. 203–204). Qutb presents the putative religious justification for this prohibition as follows.

First, he cites Qur'anic verses and a corroborating Prophetic Tradition that effectively state one should not seek knowledge from Jews and Christians (the *People of the Book*), since they are misguided and seek to misguide the Muslims (p. 204). The Qur'anic verses that Qutb refers to are the following:

Quite a number of the People of the Book wish they could Turn you (people) back to infidelity after ye have believed, from selfish envy, after the Truth hath become Manifest unto them: But forgive and overlook, Till Allah accomplish His purpose; for Allah Hath power over all things.

(2:109)

Never will the Jews or the Christians be satisfied with thee unless thou follow their form of religion. Say: "The Guidance of Allah – that is the (only) Guidance." Wert thou to follow their desires after the knowledge which hath reached thee, then wouldst thou find neither Protector nor helper against Allah.

(2:120)

O ye who believe! If ye listen to a faction among the People of the Book, they would (indeed) render you apostates after ye have believed!

(3:100)

90 *Contemporary fideism in Islam*

And the corroborating Prophetic Tradition is the following report attributed to the Prophet Muhammad:

> Inquire not from the people of the Book regarding anything. They will not lead you to the right path. They themselves are misguided. If you followed them, you would either corroborate a falsehood or falsify a truth. By God, had Moses been alive amongst you it would not have been permissible for him to adopt any other course except following me.
>
> (p. 204)

After his select quotations from Islamic sources, Qutb proceeds to reason *a fortiori* as follows: When *God Himself* has warned Muslims about the dangers of seeking guidance from Jews and Christians, it would be extremely foolish for Muslims to think that discussions about religious (Islamic) matters coming from the *People of the Book* would be based on good intentions or the sincere desire to find guidance and light (ibid).

Qutb offers a second reason as part of the religious justification he thinks shows that Muslims are prohibited from inquiring about religious matters from sources external to the Islamic faith. He does this by quoting the following part of Qur'an 2:120:

> SAY: "The Guidance of Allah – that is the (only) Guidance."

What this verse shows, he argues, is that Muslims should refer to God as the only source of guidance in religious (Islamic) matters. Deviation from Divine Guidance leads to nothing except "misguidance and aberration." Hence, there is no source of guidance and light other than God. According to Qutb, the quoted Qur'anic verse proves that "what remains after the Divine Revelation is only deviation, aberration, misguidance, deflection, and misfortune. This meaning and import of the verse is so significant that it does not admit to any doubt and discourse" (ibid).

Qutb furthers his Argument from Divine Sovereignty by offering a third reason based on the Qur'anic commandment to avoid people known to have turned away from God. He explains that the Qur'an describes such people as worshippers of "surmise and suspicion" and devoid of knowledge (p. 205). To support his point, Qutb quotes more verses from the Qur'an:

> Then withdraw (O Muhammad) from him who fleeth from Our remembrance and desireth but the life of the world. Such is their sum of knowledge. Lo! thy Lord is Best Aware of him who strayeth, and He is Best Aware of him whom goeth right.
>
> (53:29)

> They know only some appearance of the life of the world, and are heedless of the Hereafter.
>
> (30:7)

These people, who have nothing but a superficial awareness of life in this world, can only be those who are oblivious to the remembrance of God and are fond of their fleeting existence in this world. This Qur'anic description applies to "all of the scientists and expert artists of the modern age" (ibid). Because of this, it is impermissible for Muslims to acquire knowledge from such individuals about matters related to Islam. Qutb attempts to further support his case by citing yet another Qur'anic verse:

> Is he who payeth adoration in the watches of the night, prostrate and standing, bewaring of the Hereafter and hoping for the mercy of his Lord, (to be accounted equal with a disbeliever)? Say (unto them, O Muhammad): Are those who know equal with those who know not? But only men of understanding will pay heed.
>
> (39:9)

He explains that the knowledge referred to in this verse is "knowledge that guides man toward God ... not the knowledge that distorts ... human nature, and directs him on the wrong meandering path of apostasy and refusal of God" (ibid). A proper understanding of the sense in which references to knowledge are made in the Qur'an, Qutb goes on to argue, will make clear how the quoted verses are relevant to his argument:

> The sphere of knowledge is not confined to faith, religious obligations and duties, commandments and jurisprudence only. It is very wide. It is as much concerned with these laws of nature and also subjugation of those laws under the interest and purpose of the vicegerency of God, as it is with the faith and obligations and Divine laws. Of course a knowledge that has no basis in faith is outside the definition of that knowledge, to which reference has been made in the Quran and whose possessors have been praised therein.
>
> (p. 206)

For Qutb, the Qur'anic reference to knowledge is to the *entire* Divine Scheme that governs the universe and which includes truths about nature and Divine Agency as well as about faith and religious prescriptions. If this is correct, then those who 'know not', to use the Qur'anic phrase, will lack knowledge about religious matters. Therefore, in Qutb's view, it is impermissible for Muslims to try and seek knowledge from such people, based on the prohibition given in the Qur'an against following people who lack knowledge.

3.2 Reply to Qutb's Argument from Divine Sovereignty

There are multiple problems with Qutb's Argument from Divine Sovereignty. In my critical assessment of this argument, I will discuss only a few of these objections but enough to show that it is not a good argument.

92   *Contemporary fideism in Islam*

The Argument from Divine Sovereignty proceeds by drawing our attention to the Sovereignty of God. From an Islamic perspective, there is nothing objectionable about this preliminary move in the argument. Indeed, one of the Ninety-Nine Names of God in the Islamic tradition is *Malik al-Mulk* ('The King of Absolute Sovereignty'; see Qur'an 3:26). So this initial move in the argument is fine. Qutb then argues that belief in God's Sovereignty entails an acceptance of Divine Law. This also seems acceptable. From here, the argument continues as follows: Divine Law, says Qutb, is "not confined to receiving legal orders from God alone" and then acting on "judgments sought in the light of those commands." On the contrary, the Divine Law encompasses "the entire scheme that God has devised for regulating human life." Given this, Qutb infers that it is impermissible for Muslims to seek knowledge about religious matters from non-Islamic sources.

One significant assumption motivating this line of reasoning is that the Divine Law provides prescriptions on *all* matters related to regulating human life. But this does not appear to be obviously true. And Qutb's reasons for thinking that this is so seem to be based on an equivocation on the term 'Divine Law'. There are at least two ways of understanding this term. In one sense, it may be used to refer to religious prescriptions about the regulation of human life that *God has revealed*. In another sense, the term may be taken to refer to the *whole scheme devised by God for the regulation of human life*. These two interpretations of 'Divine Law' are not the same, since the latter says nothing about God's intent to reveal or disclose the Divine Scheme (at least not in its entirety).

To see this, consider the following example. A very knowledgeable doctor may know everything there is to know about the regulation of good health. In seeing a patient who is suffering from a certain ailment, say a bad cough, she may prescribe a particular treatment that consists of following a number of rules. For instance, these might include avoiding cold food and drinks, taking a cough suppressant at regular intervals and periodically gargling with warm saline solution. In disclosing this particular prescription to her patient, the doctor is not, of course, disclosing *every* bit of information that *she* knows about the regulation of good health. The patient would obviously be mistaken in thinking that the medical prescription *he* has received from the doctor exhausts all of the knowledge *the doctor* possesses about the regulation of good health. And the patient would be equally mistaken in thinking that, because the knowledgeable doctor is aware of what is required for the regulation of good health, generally speaking, *all* of this information should be (or is) disclosed to him.

Something similar can be said about God and the Divine Law. *God* may well be aware of all of the principles He has devised that regulate human life (this may be one sense in which one can speak of the 'Divine Law'), but this is not the same as His *prescribing to us* certain injunctions that are to be followed (this is another sense in which one can refer to the 'Divine Law'). Now, of course, it might be argued here that God has indeed disclosed to us

Contemporary fideism in Islam   93

all the principles that regulate human life that He is aware of. But now, note two points. First, no argument is provided by Qutb for thinking that this is the case. Second, it seems implausible to think, if one accepts the authority of the Islamic sources, that God *has* indeed done this. The Qur'an, for instance, hardly contains verses which explicitly attempt to define an ethical code of conduct. This is understandable when one sees that the Qur'an appears to assume a good deal of autonomy on our part.[26]

Here is a second objection that can be leveled against Qutb's Argument from Divine Sovereignty. Not only do the Islamic sources lack prescriptions concerning all the principles that can be said to regulate human life, they also lack any such prescriptions that can be used in support of Qutb's conclusion that it is impermissible for Muslims to acquire knowledge about religious matters from non-Islamic sources. Qutb, recall, states the following:

> A Muslim has not the authority to seek guidance and light from any other source and well-head except the Divine one in any matter that pertains to faith, the general concept of life, rituals, morals and dealings, values and standards, politics, and assembly, principles of economics, or the explanation of human history.

Let's call this proposition Q. Clearly, Q has a bearing on religious matters, since it is a claim about sources that may permissibly be consulted by Muslims about religious matters. Now, remember that whether or not something has a bearing on religious matters is, according to Qutb, the criterion that decides whether or not Muslims may permissibly rely on it as a source in seeking knowledge. But, then, one may rightly ask at this point where the appropriate references to religious (Islamic) sources are that provide the justification for Q? Since Q has a bearing on religious matters, justification in its favor must, by Qutb's own criterion, be sought from the Divine. But where does God or His Prophet explicitly state something like Q? Qutb does not cite any Islamic sources that explicitly state Q or anything close to it.

So far, we have seen that Qutb gives no good reason for thinking that the Divine Law contains prescriptions about all things related to the regulation of human life. Nor does he cite any direct evidence from religious sources in support of this claim. His conception of the Divine Law is based on confused and faulty thinking, motivated by unwarranted assumptions. Since this erroneous conception plays a crucial role in his Argument from Divine Sovereignty, Qutb's argument fails.

Let us suppose, however, for the sake of argument that the Divine Law *did* prescribe injunctions that covered all matters related to the regulation of human life. Why would this constitute a reason for thinking that seeking knowledge about these matters from external or non-Muslim sources is impermissible for committed Muslims? Qutb's response is that the domain of matters related to the regulation of human life is shared by both religion

94   Contemporary fideism in Islam

and other non-Muslim sources. As such, there is potential for conflict and indeed there is conflict between these two sources. This, Qutb maintains, may negatively impact a Muslim's faith.

In response to this worry, one can rightly ask why potential or actual conflict between Muslim and non-Muslim sources regarding truth is intrinsically problematic. After all, truth is truth, no matter where it is found.[27] No distinction is made in Islamic sources, such as the Qur'an, between different types of truth, for example, 'religious' and 'secular'. Naturally, it is a cause for concern in some sense if there is a conflict between what one takes to be two equally acceptable sources of truth. But this does not mean that one should dogmatically accept one source and discard the other. Rather than try to quarantine conflicts between Muslim and non-Muslim sources of truth, the proper – indeed, one could argue, *religious* – attitude seems to require investigation in an attempt to resolve the conflict.[28] So it seems that even if the Divine Law did prescribe injunctions that addressed all matters related to the regulation of human life, it still wouldn't straightforwardly follow that seeking knowledge about these matters from non-Muslim sources is impermissible for committed Muslims.

But aren't non-Muslim sources part of 'Jahiliyyah'? If so, shouldn't the opinions originating from these sources be viewed with suspicion by believing Muslims? The Islamic concept of 'Jahiliyyah' – 'ignorance of Divine Guidance' – features prominently in Qutb's *Milestones*. Although this concept does appear in Islamic sources,[29] Qutb uses it in an unwarranted manner by dividing the entire world into two halves – the world of Islam and the world of Jahiliyyah (consisting of all non-Muslims). To make this move requires one to make an assumption that *only* Muslims are aware (i.e., not ignorant) of Divine Guidance and that everyone else is ignorant of it. But Qutb does not provide any reason to think that this assumption is true.

One difficulty with Qutb's use of the term Jahiliyyah in an attempt to divide and classify the population of the world into the faction of Islam and that of Jahiliyyah (which includes all non-Muslims) is that it is not clear how to interpret the notion of 'Divine Guidance'. Consider the following argument that may be given in response to Qutb's use of 'Jahiliyyah'. God, according to the Qur'an, is *Al-Rahman Al-Rahim* ('Most Gracious and Most Merciful'). Given this, it seems plausible to think that He is interested in our happiness, prosperity, moral and spiritual growth, among other things. If so, one might reasonably think that Divine Guidance refers to *the obtaining of such things, and human flourishing generally speaking, along with an awareness of those principles that lead to it*. But if *this* is how we interpret Divine Guidance, then it is false that the world can be neatly divided into two parts – the world of Islam and the world of Jahiliyyah (which includes all non-Muslims). It is *clearly* false that things such as happiness, prosperity, moral and spiritual growth, etc., and knowledge of the principles that lead to the obtaining of such things, are found exclusively within the Islamic faction of the world. Not only do several non-Muslim

Contemporary fideism in Islam 95

societies exhibit several instances of human flourishing and an aware of the principles that lead to it but, in some cases, they even *excel* when compared to many Muslim societies![30] Qutb, or a defender of his position, may respond to this argument by questioning the interpretation of 'Divine Guidance' that it relies on. But this matter of interpretation is precisely the point that I think is not given due consideration by Qutb. It is not clear how to understand the concept of 'Divine Guidance' and consequently of 'Jahiliyyah'.

Finally, let me offer a few remarks in response to Qutb's putative religious justification that he believes supplements his Argument from Divine Sovereignty. Qutb maintains that there is theological warrant for the view that Muslims are not permitted to acquire knowledge from non-Muslim sources on matters that have a bearing on religious (Islamic) belief. This alleged religious justification is comprised of three basic reasons – (1) Jews and Christians are misguided and are not to be trusted, (2) the only guidance that exists is the guidance of God and (3) people who turn away from God lack knowledge about religious matters. I will address these three reasons in turn.

In response to Qutb's first reason, one can legitimately raise concerns about *which* group of Jews and Christians mentioned in the Qur'anic verses he cites are being referred to. As with any discussion where a religious scripture is referenced, context is very important. Do these verses refer to Jews and Christians *as a whole* or *a particular community* (perhaps one that existed during the time of the Prophet)? To raise this concern is response to Qutb is not *ad hoc*, for there are some references to Jews and Christians in the Qur'an that clearly cannot be taken as references to the *entire* Jewish and Christianity community. For example, Qur'an 9:30 states that the Jews maintain Ezra to be a son of God, and Qur'an 5:116 suggests that Christians regard the Trinity to be comprised of God, Jesus and Mary. Unless these verses are interpreted as referring to a *particular group* of Jews and Christians, they are obviously wrong.[31] Similarly, it remains an open question whether the reference to Jews and Christians mentioned in the Qur'anic verses and Prophetic Tradition cited by Qutb is local or universal.

As part of his second reason, Qutb appeals to Qur'an 2:120, which tersely states that the Guidance of God is the only real Guidance. I have already explained why simply appealing to the concept of Divine Guidance without any further explanation will not aid Qutb's case, so there is no need to repeat myself here.

The third reason given by Qutb is also questionable because it is not clear who specifically is being referred to in the Qur'anic verses that he cites. In these verses, God informs us to avoid people who turn away from Him, since such people lack knowledge about religious matters and whatever knowledge they have is superficial. But who are these people, exactly? We are not told. And yet Qutb, without any further explanation, informs us that

96 *Contemporary fideism in Islam*

these verses apply to "all of the scientists and expert artists of the modern age." It seems clear that Qutb's analysis of these verses is a post-facto rationalization of his conviction that they refer to present-day non-Muslims, since his interpretation does not follow from a straightforward reading of the verses in question. In one particular case, this is quite evident when Qutb cites the following verse:

> They know only some appearance of the life of the world, and are heedless of the Hereafter.
>
> (30:7)

Qutb thinks this verse clearly refers to non-Muslims. But when we read it together with the verse preceding it, which he fails to quote, this is not at all obvious:

> It is a promise of Allah. Allah faileth not His promise, but most of mankind know not. They know only some appearance of the life of the world, and are heedless of the Hereafter.
>
> (30:6–7)

Here, it is clear that the reference to those who have superficial knowledge refers to 'most of mankind', which is not the same as 'non-Muslims'. Qutb may think that the reference to 'most of mankind' in this verse is specifically about the non-Muslim population. But without any further explanation, we have no reason to think that this is the case simply based on the textual evidence offered by Qutb.

4. Some concluding remarks about contemporary fideism in Islam

The arguments in support of anti-rationalistic fideism given by contemporary Islamic thinkers such as Maududi and Qutb do not fare any better than the classical ones examined in the previous chapters. In examining the thought of these two contemporary thinkers, one can see a number of similarities between their fideistic arguments and those found in the writings of classical thinkers like Ibn Qudama and al-Ghazali (e.g., the frequent and heavy reliance on the authority of Scripture). Indeed, there is no clear distinction between classical and contemporary Islamic arguments in favor of anti-rationalistic fideism. For this reason, the writings of Ibn Qudama, al-Ghazali, Maududi and Qutb collectively provide a sufficient sample of fideistic arguments that help us understand how anti-rationalistic fideism is animated and defended in contemporary Islamic thought. But we have also seen how these arguments can be questioned and criticized. Even after a careful consideration of these arguments, then, the door remains open for a philosophical investigation of Islam.

Notes

1 For example, in response to the question whether the study of philosophy is permissible, the popular Islamic fatwa website, 'Islam QA', maintains that "[t]he majority of [Islamic] *fuqaha'* [jurists] have stated that it is *haraam* [forbidden] to study philosophy," https://islamqa.info/en/88184. Similar rulings may be found on other fatwa websites on the Internet, as well as in fatwas issued in print.

2 Yasir Qadhi, YouTube video online at www.youtube.com/watch?v=NICr4m SPVTo.

3 Ibid.

4 Ibid.

5 Amana Publications, New Edition, 1997.

6 Ibid., p. xx.

7 Ibid.

8 Ibid., p. 14.

9 Ibid., p. 868.

10 Malise Ruthven, *Islam in the World*, (New York: Oxford University Press, 2006), p. 327.

11 This paper is reprinted in Mansoor Moaddel and Kamran Talattof, *Contemporary Debates in Islam*, (New York: St. Martin's Press, 2000), pp. 207–221.

12 References to page numbers in the main text, unless stated otherwise, will be to this paper.

13 Maududi is very clear about this: "Unconditional faith is the first and foremost requirement of Islam ... [T]he moment you embrace Islam, you become a "Muslim," that is you have committed yourself to the unconditional obedience of Allah and His Prophet" (p. 218). And:

> It is not at all compatible with faith to argue and to seek justification as a condition for obedience and submission. This juxtaposition of opposites is clearly against common sense. A believer would never seek arguments and justification and whoever seeks arguments and justification cannot be a true believer.
>
> (Ibid)

14 Kenneth Cragg, *The Event of The Qur'ān*, (Oxford: Oneworld, 1994), pp. 16–19. There is, within the Islamic tradition, discussion of the 'occasions of revelation' (asbab al-nuzul) among Muslim scholars and exegetes. These are, as Farid Esack writes, "occasions ... of the revelation of a chapter or verse, which refer to the time and circumstances or place of its revelation," *The Qur'an: A Short Introduction*, (Oxford: Oneworld, 2002), p. 124. Traditional Muslim scholars maintain that, unless these occasions are referred to, certain verses in the Qur'an cannot be fully understood.

15 Shabbir Akhtar, *A Faith for All Seasons*, (Ivan R. Dee, 1991), pp. 27–28.

16 The important point to note here is that human reason may simply be taken as a *tool* to discover where ultimate authority lies. Many who criticize the practice of submitting revelation to rational scrutiny fail to appreciate this point and typically do not realize that reason need not be inflated to the point where it is personified and revered as a *person* or an *idol*.

17 Muhammad Asad, *The Message of The Qur'ān*, (Gibraltar: Dar Al-Andalus, 1980), p. 12.

18 See Chapter 3.

19 Peter R. Demant, *Islam vs. Islamism: The Dilemma of the Muslim World*, (Westport: Praeger, 2006), p. 98.

20 Ibid.

21 Ibid., pp. 98–99.

98 *Contemporary fideism in Islam*

22 Roxanne L. Euben, *Enemy in the Mirror: Islamic Fundamentalism and the Limits of Modern Rationalism*, (Princeton: Princeton University Press, 1999), p. 67.

23 Ibid., p. 70.

24 I will be referring to the excerpt from *Milestones* published as 'Islam as The Foundation of Knowledge', in Moaddel and Talatoff, *op. cit.* Subsequent references to page numbers in the main text, unless stated otherwise, will be to this work.

25 The word 'Jahiliyyah' refers roughly to the Islamic concept of 'ignorance of Divine Guidance'. The reference to Jahiliyyah is central in Qutb's development of his theological outlook in *Milestones*. Euben explains this term, and the context in which it is used by Qutb, as follows:

> *Jahiliyya*, a term taken directly from the Qur'an, specifically refers to the period of pre-Islamic ignorance in Arabia. As revived by [Maududi], and subsequently used by Qutb, *jahiliyya* becomes a condition rather than a particular historical period, a state of ignorance into which society descends whenever it deviates from the Islamic way. Whereas ancient *jahiliyya* was a function of simple ignorance, modern *jahiliyya* is a conscious usurpation of God's authority. All contemporary ills are the product of this foundational transgression of human hubris.
>
> (Euben, *op. cit.*, p. 57)

26 As Khaled Abou El Fadl writes on the topic of the Qur'an and ethics:

> The Qur'an itself refers to general moral imperatives such as mercy, justice, kindness, or goodness. The Qur'an does not clearly define any of these categories, but presumes a certain amount of moral probity on [the] part of the reader. For instance, the Qur'an persistently commands Muslims [to] enjoin the good. The word used for "the good" is *ma'ruf*, which means that which is commonly known to be good. Goodness, in the Qur'anic discourse, is part of what one may call a lived reality – it is the product of human experience, and constructed normative understandings,
>
> 'The Place of Tolerance in Islam', in Joshua Cohen and Ian Lague (eds.), *The Place of Tolerance in Islam*, (Boston: Beacon Press, 2002), p. 14. For a more detailed case in favor of supposing that the Qur'ān may be read as allowing for autonomy on our part with respect to moral deliberation, see George F. Hourani, *Reason and Tradition in Islamic Ethics*, (Cambridge: Cambridge University Press, 1985), pp. 43–45. Hourani presents four considerations he thinks jointly suggest that "the Qur'ān allows for independent ethical judgement by man".
>
> (ibid)

27 As Al-Kindi famously writes:

> We ought not to be ashamed of appreciating the truth and of acquiring it wherever it comes from, even if it comes from races distant and nations different from us. For the seeker of truth nothing takes precedence over the truth, and there is no disparagement of the truth, nor belittling either of him who speaks it or of him who conveys it. (The status of) no one is diminished by the truth; rather does the truth ennoble us all,
>
> Alfred L. Ivry, *Al-Kindi's Metaphysics: A Translation of Ya'qūb ibn Ishāq al-Kindī's Treatise 'On First Philosophy'*, (Albany: State University of New York Press, 1974), p. 58.

28 For, one might reasonably say, "all truth is God's truth." In other words, if God is indeed the Author of every facet of the world in which we live, then there

Contemporary fideism in Islam 99

cannot be any discrepancy between bona fide Divine Revelation and authentic knowledge regarding other aspects of human life. The phrase "all truth is God's truth" forms the title of a book by Arthur F. Holmes, in which he discusses the implications of this statement in further detail. See his *All Truth Is God's Truth*, (Grand Rapids: Eerdmans Publishing Co., 1977).

29 The term 'Jahiliyyah' appears in only a few instances in the Qur'an (e.g., 5:50; 33:33), and it is not at all obvious how to understand it based on its brief mention in Scripture.

30 Many Muslim immigrants to Western countries migrate there because of what they regard as the better quality of living in general and a greater respect for human rights (e.g., freedom of religious belief, gender equality, etc.). For more on this, and other matters related to Muslim immigration to Western countries, see Yvonne Yazbeck Haddad and Jane I. Smith (eds.), *Muslim Minorities in the West*, (Walnut Creek: Altamira Press, 2002).

31 Regarding the Qur'anic claim about the Jews believing Ezra to be a son of God, George Sale writes:

> This grievous charge against the Jews the commentators endeavour to support by telling us that it is meant of *some ancient heterodox Jews*, or else of *some Jews of Medina*; who said so for no other reason than for that the law being utterly lost and forgotten during the Babylonish captivity, Ezra, having being raised to life after he had been dead one hundred years, ... dictated the whole anew to the scribes, out of his own memory; at which they greatly marveled, and declared that he could not have done it unless he were the son of God.
>
> (Italics mine)

See his *The Koran*, (London: Frederick Warne and Co. Ltd, 1909), p. 183. And as for the Qur'an's reference to the Christian Trinity being comprised of God, Jesus and Mary, Sale explains that a number of commentators "mention *a sect of Christians* which held the Trinity to be composed of those three [i.e., God, Jesus and Mary]; but it is allowed that this heresy has been long since extinct," p. 96. Italics mine.

5 Rationalist arguments for Islamic belief

1. A philosophical investigation of Islam

After having invested a fair amount of time critically exploring and ultimately rejecting fideism as a barrier to a philosophical investigation of Islam, it is now time to attend to the investigation itself. What does a philosophical investigation of Islam yield? As explained in the Preface, to investigate Islam philosophically primarily involves an assessment of rationalist arguments that may be given to support the truth of Islamic belief. The core of Islamic belief is encapsulated in the *shahadah*, the Islamic testimony of faith, which states that there is no god but God (Allah) and that Muhammad is His Messenger. A Muslim is someone who assents to the truth of these two propositions, viz. (1) 'God exists' and (2) 'Muhammad is God's Messenger'. On this matter, there is no real controversy among Muslim thinkers.[1] Based on this, I shall deem a rationalist case for Islamic belief to be successful if there are good rationalist arguments in favor of God's existence as well as for the Prophethood of Muhammad.

1.1 Rationalist arguments for the existence of god

Since the religious context that informs the present discussion about rationalist arguments for God's existence is specifically an Islamic one, I will concentrate on those arguments for the existence of God that were predominantly discussed in the history of Islamic thought. The Qur'an generally refers to the origins of the universe and its apparent design and order as evidence of God's existence (see, for example, 52:35–36; 78:6–16). These references form the basis of the two main types of arguments that have been discussed in Islamic philosophical thought – Cosmological and Design Arguments.[2] Whether these arguments are successful is controversial and philosophers of religion continue to debate them today. In what follows, I will highlight two fundamental problems facing those who want to use these arguments to provide a rationalist vindication of Islamic belief.

(i) **Controversial premises and principles:** The goal of a rationalist argument for God's existence, a 'theistic proof' as Stephen T. Davis calls it, is to

Rationalist arguments for Islamic belief 101

substantiate the theist's belief in God, give a good reason for it, show that it is credible, show that it is true ... [T]heistic proofs ... try to demonstrate the rationality of theistic belief to *all rational persons* (whoever exactly they are).[3]

A proper understanding of this goal of rationalist arguments reveals an important condition that must be met if such arguments are to succeed. Davis explains:

It is crucial that the premises of a successful theistic proof be known to be more plausible than their denials ... by any rational person; and ideally they must be known by the people to whom the rationality of belief in the existence of God is to be demonstrated ... If the premises of a theistic proof are more plausible than their denials but the relevant people do not know that fact, the rationality of theism will not be demonstrated to them. Neither believers nor unbelievers in the existence of God will receive the intended benefit, namely, recognition of the rationality of belief in the existence of God.[4]

It is precisely with respect to this critical condition that many formulations of the Cosmological and Design Arguments fail. The premises of these arguments rely on controversial *a priori* principles that are typically contested by those who do not believe in God. Consider, as one example to illustrate the point, the Leibnizian version of the Cosmological Argument according to which there is a Sufficient Reason (God) why there is something instead of nothing.[5] This version of the argument hinges critically on the 'principle of sufficient reason', which, as Alexander R. Pruss explains, basically states that "[e]verything that is the case must have reason why it is the case."[6] But critics of Cosmological Arguments have tended to question this sort of *a priori* principle. J. L. Mackie, for example, in a frequently quoted passage cited in discussions of Cosmological Arguments, objects to the Leibnizian formulation as follows:

The principle of sufficient reason expresses a demand that things should be intelligible *through and through*. The simple reply to the argument which relies on it is that there is nothing that justifies this demand, and nothing that supports the belief that it is satisfiable even in principle ... The form of the cosmological argument which relies on the principle of sufficient reason therefore fails completely as a demonstrative proof.[7]

Mackie's objection here does not seem unreasonable. But if it is not unreasonable, then it follows, as he himself notes, that the Leibnizian Cosmological Argument is unsuccessful. The challenge for those who want to vindicate Islamic or theistic belief based on some version of the Cosmological or Design Argument is to formulate the argument in such a way that *all* its premises (including any *a priori* ones) are generally known to be more

102 *Rationalist arguments for Islamic belief*

plausible than their denials. To my knowledge, no Cosmological or Design Argument of this sort exists.

(ii) Theoretical insufficiency: Suppose, however, that a version of the Cosmological or Design Argument can be formulated that does not rely on controversial premises or principles. Given that Cosmological and Design Arguments usually do not go beyond the conclusion that a 'first cause' or 'intelligent designer' exists, these arguments fail in demonstrating the existence of *God* as traditionally conceived. In his *Jerusalem Epistle*, al-Ghazali provides a helpful summary of the fundamental doctrines of Islamic orthodoxy.[8] In commenting specifically on knowledge of the attributes of God, he writes:

> [Knowledge of God's attributes] comprises ten fundamentals, namely the knowledge that He is living ... all-knowing ... all-powerful ... all-willing ... all-hearing ... all-seeing ... and speaking ..., but is exalted above and immune from incorporation in phenomena; and that His speech, knowledge, and will are pre-existent and eternal.[9]

It is difficult to see how one can further infer these attributes simply from the existence of some 'first cause' or 'intelligent designer'. How would one know, for instance, that such a being is all-hearing or that it is 'immune from incorporation in phenomena' (i.e., not a physical being)? Proponents of Cosmological and Design Arguments usually forego attempts to answer such questions. As William Lane Craig comments, after a sustained defense of the 'kalam' version of the Cosmological Argument,

> The kalām cosmological argument leads us to a personal Creator of the universe, but as to whether this Creator is omniscient, good, perfect, and so forth, we shall not inquire. These questions are logically posterior to the question of His existence. But if our argument is sound and a personal Creator of the universe really does exist, then surely it is incumbent upon us to inquire whether He has specially revealed Himself to man in some way that we might know Him more fully or whether, like Aristotle's unmoved mover, He remains aloof and detached from the world that He has made.[10]

But in making such a concession, one is effectively admitting that the existence of *God* has not been demonstrated. William Rowe is thus right to criticize Cosmological Arguments as follows:

> [I]f the cosmological argument purports to establish the existence of the theistic God when in fact it, at best, establishes the existence of a first efficient cause or a necessary being, then the argument is obviously a failure ... Why must a first efficient cause or a necessary being have the properties of the theistic God?[11]

Rationalist arguments for Islamic belief   103

This sort of objection is not new. In David Hume's *Dialogues Concerning Natural Religion*, Philo responds to Cleanthes' presentation of the Design Argument by noting that the argument would at best prove the existence of some sort of intelligent agency behind the creation of the universe. "But beyond that position," Philo famously objects, the defender of such an argument "cannot ascertain one single circumstance, and is left afterwards to fix every point of his theology, by the utmost license of fancy and hypothesis."[12]

1.2 Rationalist arguments for the Prophethood of Muhammad

Do rationalist arguments for the Prophethood of Muhammad fare any better than those for the existence of God discussed above? The classic Islamic argument for the Prophethood of Muhammad centers on the miraculous nature of the Qur'an. Andrew Rippin explains the early genesis of this argument and summarizes it as follows:

> It would appear that, early on, Muslims had to defend their nascent religion against Christian theological attack in the area of the Fertile Crescent, especially Iraq. The following argument was constructed: miracles prove the status of Prophethood and the Qur'an is Muhammad's miracle; therefore, Muhammad was truly a prophet and Islam is a true, revealed religion. All participants in the debate appear to have agreed on the first premise. What Muslims had to prove, and Christians disprove, was the validity [*sic*] of the second, for the conclusion, the truth of Islam, stood or fell on its credibility. Over time, the argument became one concerned to prove the "inimitability" of the Qur'an, an argument which, its proponents were quick to point out, had a basis in the Qur'an itself ... [T]he production of a text "like" the Qur'an is encouraged but known to be impossible: "Produce a sūra like it [i.e. the Qur'an], and call on whom you can, besides God, if you speak truthfully" (Qur'an 10/38); "Well then bring ten chapters the like of it, forged!" (Qur'an 11/13). God has given the Qur'an to Muhammad and because of its divine origin, no text "like" it can, in fact, be produced. The inimitability of the text proves its divine authorship and thus its status as a miracle, confirming Muhammad's role and the veracity of Islam.[13]

According to Issa J. Boullata, Muslim consensus maintains that the inimitability of the Qur'anic text refers mainly to its *stylistic* supremacy, which is held to be especially remarkable given that the Qur'anic revelation was preached by Muhammad, an illiterate man.[14] Muslim tradition maintains that this challenge to produce something like the Qur'an has never been successfully met since it was first raised. This alleged fact is offered as strong evidence for the divine origin of the Qur'an and the Prophethood of Muhammad. One advantage that the 'Argument from Qur'anic Inimitability' has

104   *Rationalist arguments for Islamic belief*

over the sort of rationalist arguments for God's existence discussed above is that it can get around the problem of theoretical insufficiency in the following way. Suppose that the Qur'an is indeed 'inimitable' and that this fact constitutes a miracle. If one grants the plausible assumption that miracles prove the status of Prophethood, one would then have good evidence for thinking that Muhammad is indeed God's Prophet. And if that is so, then one would also have good evidence for taking seriously what Muhammad says about God, including his views about the nature of the divine. But does the Argument from Qur'anic Inimitability succeed? I don't think that it does.

One problem with the argument is that the concept of a 'miracle' it relies on is not the classical one we find in Hume. Hume's famous definition of a miracle in his essay 'Of Miracles' see a miracle as "a transgression of a law of nature by a particular volition of the Deity, or by the interposition of some invisible agent."[15] But as Ibn Rushd notes in his *Incoherence of the Incoherence*, the miracle of the Qur'an does not involve

> an interruption in the course of nature ... like the changing of a rod into a serpent, but ... is established by way of perception and consideration for every man who has been or will be till the day of resurrection.[16]

Arguably, the occurrence of a miracle in the Humean sense does provide some evidence for the occurrence of supernatural activity. For, it seems that only something like God could explain the violation of a law of nature that is confirmed to hold universally. But if an alleged miracle does not violate any laws of nature, then it becomes difficult to ascertain its evidential value. This point is behind Richard Swinburne's basic objection to the Islamic claim that the Qur'an is miraculous. "We have no reason to suspect that that illiterate creative genius cannot guess at truths normally accessible only to the literate," he says, "or create a new religious style or movement."[17] The claim that the text of the Qur'an is stylistically imitable is an aesthetic judgment, and it is controversial whether such judgments are objective and can be evaluated according to objective criteria.[18] It is also controversial what kind of aesthetic merit in a work is a mark of divine inspiration. No traditional Muslim would regard the Vedas to be divine in origin, despite the claim by some Hindu thinkers that they must be so because of their 'inimitability'.[19] But why not? What aesthetic difference is there between the Qur'an and the ancient Hindu scriptures such that the text of the former counts as divine revelation whereas the latter does not? It is difficult to see how one can answer this question without avoiding subjective aesthetic judgments. The fact that, outside of the Muslim community, there is no consensus among speakers of Arabic regarding the stylistic inimitability of the Qur'an further supports this point. Rippin is thus correct in describing the Argument from Qur'anic Inimitability as a "dogmatic one, essential to the proof of the status of the text, but one which operates (like many other religious arguments) within the presuppositions of Islam alone."[20]

2. Prospects for a rationalist case for Islamic belief

My treatment of rationalist arguments for the existence of God and the Prophethood of Muhammad has admittedly been brief, but sufficient I hope to draw attention to some serious obstacles that must be overcome before Islamic belief can be rationally vindicated. The brevity of my assessment is also due in part to the absence of any substantive philosophical offerings from the Muslim community today to show that Islamic belief is true or rational to hold. Part of the reason for this is the predominance of fideism, which I have addressed in previous chapters. Many Muslims also seem to think that Islamic belief, if not self-evident to all, is evident enough to forego any serious rationalist attempt at justification. As Frithjof Schuon explains,

> The intellectual - and thereby the rational - foundation of Islam results in the average Muslim having a curious tendency to believe that non-Muslims either know that Islam is the truth and reject it out of pure obstinacy, or else are simply ignorant of it and can be converted by elementary explanations; that anyone should be able to oppose Islam with a good conscience quite exceeds the Muslim's imagination, precisely because Islam coincides in his mind with the irresistible logic of things.[21]

Schuon's point about the tendency of the average Muslim to offer 'elementary explanations' in an attempt to justify his or her faith is also noted by W. Montgomery Watt, who makes the following observation about the traditionalist Muslim mind-set:

> Traditionalist Muslims today like to claim that 'Islam is a religion based on reason'; but if asked to elaborate this point, they can only produce the sort of philosophical reasoning that was in vogue in the twelfth century ... [T]hey know of no philosophy since Averroes, and are completely unaware of the new challenges to religious belief produced by men like Hume and Feuerbach, not to mention our twentieth-century [now twenty-first century] philosophers.[22]

A rationalist vindication of Islamic belief will need to show that belief in the existence of God (as understood in Islam) as well as the Prophethood of Muhammad is reasonable to hold. This is not an easy task, given some of the problems noted in the preceding section. Moreover, many people living in our current secular climate, informed by science, history, philosophy, etc., are very skeptical of religious claims, such as the ones we find in the Islamic religion, and raise a variety of objections to religious belief. Here, I want to briefly note some of these objections that will have to be dealt with by thinkers interested in rationally vindicating Islamic belief (in no particular order):

(1) The problem of religious diversity: Those Muslims who encounter other religious traditions may start to wonder whether their specific beliefs about

106 *Rationalist arguments for Islamic belief*

the existence of God, the nature of the Divine, eschatology, etc., are true. As William P. Alston notes, the diversity in and mutual incompatibilities among beliefs about religion "poses a serious and well advertised problem for the claims of each community."[23] "After all," writes Alston, "*it looks as if* Moslems [*sic*], Hindus, and Buddhists have grounds of the same general sort (revelation, religious experience, miracles, authority, etc.) as my fellow Christians and I have for the truth of our respective systems of doctrine."[24] If this is the case, then it does appear that we have a problem. Alston goes on to explain:

> But then, unless I have sufficient reason for supposing that Christians are in a superior position for discerning the truth about these matters, why should I suppose that we are right and they are wrong? How can I be justified in continuing to affirm my Christian beliefs?[25]

Now, of course, traditional Muslims will offer their own Islamic interpretation of religious diversity, for example, all non-Islamic religions today are corruptions of varying degrees of God's original religion of Islamic monotheism. But such an explanation of religious diversity, being 'internal' to Islam, is clearly controversial and will not be plausible to anyone who is not already a committed Muslim. The challenge to the Muslim is to explain why his account of religious diversity is preferable to all other competing accounts.

(2) The challenge of historical criticism: The traditional Muslim account of the origins of Islam as a historical religion has especially been challenged since the 19th century. As F. E. Peters explains, commenting on the famous words of the French historian Ernest Renan that Islam was 'born in full view of history':

> Within twenty-five years after Ernest Renan wrote those words, his optimism regarding Islamic origins – or perhaps simply his pessimism at getting at the historical Jesus – already stood in need of serious revision. History's view of the birth of Islam, it turned out, was neither particularly clear, and the search after Islamic origins had to begin where the search for Christianity's origins had, standing before the evidence for the life of the founder and its mileu.[26]

It is controversial whether the available historical evidence supports the traditional Muslim account of Islamic origins.[27] A rationalist vindication of Islamic belief would have to take this evidence seriously and argue that, despite claims to the contrary, it does indeed point to the truth of the traditional Muslim account. Unfortunately, many Muslims, including several scholars, do not take the claims and methods of historical criticism seriously. For example, in what can only be described as a muddled, dogmatic dismissal of historical criticism and Islam, the Islamic philosopher Seyyed Hossein Nasr states:

> The acceptance of the Koran as the word of God suggests that the so-called historical and textual study of the Koran is tantamount to

questioning the historical existence of Jesus Christ, as some people in the West have claimed. The rules of biblical criticism do not apply to the Koran as God's revelation, because what corresponds to the Bible is the hadith collection, which comprises the words and deeds of the Prophet of Islam as the Bible comprises the words and deeds of Jesus Christ. Both the hadith books and the Bible were compiled after the revelation, whereas the Koran has existed in its present form from the very beginning of Islamic revelation. To claim that the so-called history of the Koran undermines or casts doubt on its being a divine revelation is not only to misunderstand the nature of the Koran but also to go against the historical evidence.[28]

Nasr effectively repudiates the applicability of the methods of historical criticism to Islam because the Qur'an is (to his mind) first and foremost a divine revelation. His response here is reminiscent of a similar dogmatic remark by the Swiss Reformed theologian Karl Barth, who on a particular occasion was having a discussion with another theologian, D. T. Niles, about non-Christian faiths. When asked by Niles how he knew that Hinduism constituted unbelief without ever having met a Hindu person, Barth answered that he knew this *a priori*.[29]

(3) The Problem of Evil: One strange fact about contemporary Islamic thought is that Muslim thinkers do not really engage with The Problem of Evil, while it constitutes a serious area of discussion in Judeo-Christian Philosophy of Religion. Many Jewish and Christian thinkers continue to grapple with this problem, which the Catholic theologian Hans Küng calls the "rock of atheism."[30] By contrast, there is an absence of Muslim voices in the discussion, as Shabbir Akhtar notes:

> Islamic thought does not concede as fundamental the problem of evil (and the associated problem of the overwhelming amount of suffering it causes) in a universe created and ruled by a good and omnipotent God. No Muslim thinker or educated layman has identified theodicy as a project worthy of elaborate consideration. And yet, among western philosophers of religion, the problem of evil takes a place at least as prominent as the problem of proving God's very existence.[31]

The reason this is strange is because the ingredients that give rise to The Problem of Evil are all present in Islam, as they are in Judaism and Christianity. Virtually all Muslims hold God to be good and omnipotent. They also believe in the reality of evil (*sharr*). Indeed, there are additional theological components in Islamic belief that serve to *amplify* The Problem of Evil. God is held to be the author of evil, for instance (Qur'an 113:2). Many Muslim thinkers have also rejected the idea of free will, which most contemporary theistic philosophers of religion appeal to in arguing for the compatibility of God's existence and 'moral evil' in our world – evil that arises from the

108 *Rationalist arguments for Islamic belief*

(mis)use of human freedom.[32] In a creedal statement attributed to Ahmad ibn Hanbal we read the following:

> Man's destiny is from God, with its good and evil, its paucity and abundance, its outward and inward, its sweet and bitter, its liked and disliked, its good and bad, its first and last [that is, every aspect of human life]. It is a decree that He has ordained, a destiny that He has determined for men. No one ever will go beyond the will of God (may He be glorified), nor overstep His decree. Rather, all will attain the destiny for which He has created them, applying themselves to the deeds which He has determined for them in His justice (may our Lord be glorified) …[33]

Ibn Hanbal further states that Satan and others who disobey God were created for that disobedience. Similarly, God created those who are obedient to Him for that obedience.[34] Without any further explanation or argument, it is hard to see how one could coherently regard God as wholly good, omnipotent and the creator of our world *as well as* all its evils. The Muslim theodicist has his task cut out for him.

(4) **The moral objection to Islamic belief:** A final objection against the rationality of Islamic belief that I will consider here involves the moral implications of accepting it. This objection, a very common one voiced in Western societies, goes something like this. Accepting Islamic belief means involving oneself in Islamic practice. But certain things in Islamic practice are morally objectionable. Because one should not do things that are morally objectionable, one should not accept Islamic belief. This sort of objection can be applied in a theoretical manner against the truth or reasonableness of Islamic belief. God, who is by definition wholly good, cannot command things that are immoral. Since Islam appears to teach things that are immoral, the Islamic faith cannot be based on a true revelation from God. Some commonly cited examples of morally objectional Islamic practices include waging war against unbelievers (see, for example, Qur'an 9:5), the permission given to a man to beat his wife to discipline her (Qur'an 4:34), punishing those guilty of fornication with a hundred lashes (Qur'an 2:42) and killing or crucifying those who wage war against God and His Messenger to cause corruption in the land (Qur'an 5:33). Several other examples can be produced from the *ahadith*, but there is no need to cite them here.

Muslim thinkers who have tried to defend the reasonableness of Islamic belief in response to the moral objection have offered a few different replies. One reply appeals to the divine command theory of ethics, according to which what makes an action right or wrong is simply the fact that it is commanded or forbidden by God. By defending this ethical theory, and rejecting those from which the moral objection to Islamic belief stems, some Muslims have held there is no legitimate basis from which an 'external' moral critique of Islam may be given. Other replies question the alleged immorality of the cited Islamic practices, either by arguing that the textual references to them must be understood in a historical context (e.g., the 'sword verse' of 9:5 is said to refer only to a certain group of pagan Arabs of Muhammad's time) or else that the textual references have been misinterpreted (e.g., the reference to wife beating in the Qur'an is supposed to be symbolic only).

All of these replies are controversial and raise further difficulties. The divine command theory is generally rejected by contemporary philosophers and ethicists, usually for reasons that were noted by Plato in his dialogue *Euthyphro*. The claim that certain morally objectionable Islamic injunctions must be understood in a historical context is not agreed upon by Muslim thinkers. But even if these injunctions are historically confined to Muhammad's time, this does not solve the problem of how one can regard these as being commanded by a wholly good God. As for issues surrounding interpretation, if morally objectionable injunctions in the Qur'an can be avoided only by a circuitous rejection of literalism, one wonders why God's revealed Scripture contains them in the first place. Most Muslims take religious injunctions literally and seriously, such as religious directives to pray, fast, refrain from adultery, etc. The attempt to render symbolic only those Islamic injunctions that are immoral appears to be *ad hoc*, done to safeguard the traditionalist Muslim belief that there is nothing wrong with them.

3. Some concluding remarks about my philosophical investigation of Islam

Here, then, are the results of a philosophical investigation of Islamic belief. Based on the points covered in this chapter, the prospects for a rationalist vindication of the truth of Islamic belief seem unlikely. To maintain otherwise would require a sustained rationalist effort in providing good arguments for the existence of God as well as for the Prophethood of Muhammad. It would also require a defense of Islamic belief against some of the challenges to it that I have noted. A helpful example of what would be required for a rationalist vindication of the truth of Islamic belief can be seen in the works of Richard Swinburne. Although Swinburne's work focuses on the Christian religion, it is his approach to religious matters that is illustrative here. Arguably, Swinburne's work in the Philosophy of Religion constitutes the best contemporary philosophical case for Christian belief.[35] His case can be broadly divided into two parts. The first part of Swinburne's case is found in his works *The Coherence of Theism*, *The Existence of God* and *Faith and Reason*,[36] in which he deals with 'generic' theism. In this trilogy, like most theistic philosophers of religion, Swinburne argues for the coherence and epistemic justifiability of belief in God, as understood in classical Judaism, Christianity and Islam. The second part of Swinburne's case focuses in the specific claims of the Christian religion and is comprised of the tetralogy *Responsibility and Atonement*, *Revelation*, *The Christian God* and *Providence and The Problem of Evil*.[37] In this tetralogy, Swinburne makes a case for some of the core doctrines of Christianity, such as the doctrines

110   *Rationalist arguments for Islamic belief*

of Atonement and the Trinity. Taken all together, these seven works, as William Hasker puts it, "constitute a sustained defence of the coherence and plausibility of the orthodox Christian faith."[38] As far as I am aware, no comparable effort is to be found among contemporary Muslim thinkers.

Notes

1 Assenting to the truth of God's existence and the Prophethood of Muhammad is at least *necessary* for a person to be a Muslim, according to virtually all Muslim thinkers. Whether it is also *sufficient* is controversial.
2 In his work *Islamic Thought on the Existence of God*, (The Council for Research Values in Philosophy, 2003), Cafer S. Yaran divides the Islamic arguments for the existence of God into three categories – (i) The Argument from Religious Experience, (ii) Teleological Arguments and (iii) Cosmological Arguments (see his table of contents). His discussion of the Argument from Religious Experience is brief, after which the rest of the book is mainly a critical examination of Design and Cosmological Arguments. For a useful survey of the arguments in Islamic thought that were used to support belief in the existence of God, see Majid Fakhry, 'The Classical Islamic Arguments for the Existence of God', *The Muslim World*, 47, (1957), pp. 133–145.
3 Stephen T. Davis, *God, Reason and Theistic Proofs*, (Edinburgh: Edinburgh University Press, 1997), p. 6. Italics mine.
4 Ibid., 7.
5 William Lane Craig, 'The Cosmological Argument', in Paul Copan and Paul K. Moser (eds.), *The Rationality of Theism*, (London: Routledge, 2003), p. 114.
6 Alexander R. Pruss, *The Principle of Sufficient Reason: A Reassessment*, (Cambridge: Cambridge University Press, 2010), p. 3.
7 J. L. Mackie, *The Miracle of Theism*, (Oxford: Oxford University Press, 1982), pp. 85–87.
8 Trans. A. L. Tibawi, 'Al-Ghazali's Tract on Dogmatic Theology', *The Islamic Quarterly* 9, 3/4 (1965), pp. 65–122.
9 Ibid., pp. 95–96.
10 William Lane Craig, *The Kalām Cosmological Argument*, (London: Macmillan, 1979), pp. 152–153.
11 William Rowe, *The Cosmological Argument*, (Princeton: Princeton University Press, 1975), p. 5.
12 David Hume, *Dialogues Concerning Natural Religion* [1779], ed. Martin Bell, (Harmondsworth: Penguin, 1990), p. 79.
13 Andrew Rippin, *Muslims: Their Religious Beliefs and Practices*, Third Edition, (London: Routledge, 2005), p. 38.
14 Issa J. Boullata, 'The Rhetorical Interpretation of the Qur'an: I'jaz and Related Topics', in Andrew Rippin (ed.), *Approaches to the History of the Interpretations of the Qur'an*, (Oxford: Clarendon Press, 1988), p. 142.
15 David Hume, 'Of Miracles', *An Enquiry Concerning Human Understanding*, www.bartleby.com/37/3/14.html.
16 Ibn Rushd, Simon van den Bergh, (trans.), *Averroes' Tahafut Al-Tahafut*, (London: Trustees of the E. J. W. Gibb Memorial, 1978), p. 315.
17 Richard Swinburne, *Revelation: From Metaphor to Analogy*, Second Edition, (Oxford: Oxford University Press, 2007), p. 128.
18 See Oliver Leaman, *Islamic Aesthetics: An Introduction*, (Notre Dame: University of Notre Dame Press, 2004), p. 142.
19 Commenting on the Upanishads, scriptures that are part of the Vedas, the Indian thinker Sri Aurobindo describes them as "documents of revelatory and

Rationalist arguments for Islamic belief 111

intuitive philosophy of an inexhaustible light, power and largeness and, whether written in verse or cadenced prose, spiritual poems of an absolute, an unfailing inspiration inevitable in phrase, wonderful in rhythm and expression," 'The Upanishads', www.hinduwebsite.com/divinelife/auro/auro_upanishads.asp.

20 Rippin, *Muslims: Their Religious Beliefs and Practices*, pp. 39–40.

21 Frithjof Schuon, *Stations of Wisdom*, (Bloomington: World Wisdom Books, 1961), p. 64, note 1.

22 W. Montgomery Watt, *Islamic Fundamentalism and Modernity*, (London: Routledge, 1988), p. 5.

23 William P. Alston, 'Religious Diversity and Perceptual Knowledge of God', in Philip L. Quinn and Kevin Meeker (eds.), *The Philosophical Challenge of Religious Diversity*, (New York: Oxford University Press, 2000), p. 193.

24 Ibid. Italics mine.

25 Ibid.

26 F. E. Peters, 'The Quest of the Historical Muhammad', *International Journal of Middle East Studies*, 23.3 (1991), p. 292.

27 For a useful survey of some of the controversies surrounding this evidence, see Toby Lester, 'What Is the Koran?', *The Atlantic*, January 1999, www.theatlantic. com/magazine/archive/1999/01/what-is-the-koran/304024/.

28 Seyyed Hossein Nasr, 'Letters', *The Atlantic*, April 1999, www.theatlantic.com/ magazine/archive/1999/04/letters/377566/.

29 As cited in David H. Jensen, *Always Being Reformed: Challenges and Prospects for the Future of Reformed Theology*, (Eugene: Pickwick Publications, 2016), p. 79.

30 Hans Kung, *On Being a Christian*, trans. Edward Quinn, (New York: Doubleday, 1976), p. 432.

31 Shabbir Akhtar, *The Quran and the Secular Mind*, p. 82.

32 For a classic treatment, see Alvin Plantinga, *God, Freedom and Evil*, (Grand Rapids: William B. Eerdmans Publishing Company, 1974).

33 Ibn Hanbal, Tabaqat al-Hanabilah, in Kenneth Cragg & R. Marston Speight, *Islam from Within: An Anthology of a Religion*, (Belmont: Wadsworth Publishing Co., 1980), p. 120.

34 Ibid.

35 As Brian Hebblethwaite writes,

> Richard Swinburne ... [has] raised the standard and increased the plausibility of natural theology to new levels. Swinburne, in addition, is advancing the cause of rational theology – the philosophical articulation and defense of the main articles of Christian doctrine – with a high degree of professional expertise ... [T]heologians can hardly afford to ignore the kind of philosophical defense of Christian doctrine with the degree of professional skill that Swinburne shows.

See Hebblethwaite's article 'The Anglican Tradition', in Philip L. Quinn and Charles Taliaferro (eds.), *A Companion to Philosophy of Religion*, (Cambridge: Blackwell Publishers, 1997), pp. 176–177.

36 All published by Oxford University Press (Clarendon Press) in 1977, 1979 and 1981, respectively.

37 All published by Oxford University Press (Clarendon Press) in 1989, 1992, 1994 and 1998, respectively.

38 See William Hasker, 'Is Christianity probable? Swinburne's apologetic programme', *Religious Studies*, 38, (2002), p. 253.

6 Religious doubt, Islamic faith and the Skeptical Muslim

1. Doubts about Islamic belief

The conclusions of my philosophical investigation of Islam in the preceding chapter mean that there are reasonable grounds for doubting Islamic belief. In this final chapter, I want to explore the possibility of a person remaining a Muslim despite harboring doubts about his or her faith. Although my discussion here deals specifically with religious doubt in an Islamic context, a fair amount of what I say applies more generally to matters of religious doubt and religious faith.

My own interest in this topic stems mainly from concerns about the *practical* ramifications of the view that religious doubt and Islamic faith are incompatible. Consider, for instance, how Muslims who hold such a view may think that the only appropriate course of action is to abandon their religious commitment and stop referring to themselves as 'Muslim', upon finding themselves in a state of religious doubt. This sort of move may be welcomed by (some) members of the Muslim community who feel that religious doubters have no place in it. Indeed, people who are seen as expressing religious doubts about Islam, whether they are Muslim or non-Muslim, may be – and certainly have been – shunned, ostracized, persecuted, punished or even killed. Many real-life examples of these sorts of things can be given, but let me confine myself to a few recent cases that featured in news reports.

On 21 January 2015, Wan Sulaiman, a Malaysian businessman, had his home raided by the local religious authorities, who confiscated his personal notes and screened his personal computer and mobile phone. The same day, he was charged with "mocking, ridiculing or insulting Quranic or hadith texts." The charge appears to have arisen simply because Sulaiman sought clarification from religious authorities regarding differences among Muslims on matters of Islamic rituals, like the *shahada* (declaration of Islamic faith).[1] According to one news report, Sulaiman got himself into trouble with the religious authorities mainly because of his "fondness of asking questions, especially about Islam, the very religion that he practises."[2] In another, more well-known case, the Saudi government began administering

Religious doubt and the Skeptical Muslim 113

its punishment of 1,000 lashes and ten years in prison on Raif Badawi, a Saudi activist and blogger, starting 9 January 2015. Even though, according to him, he is no critic or enemy of Islam, Badawi nevertheless criticized the religiopolitical aspects of the Saudi-Wahhabi establishment.[3] Here is a specimen from his writings:

> As soon as a thinker starts to reveal his ideas, you will find hundreds of fatwas that accused him of being an infidel just because he had the courage to discuss some sacred topics. I'm really worried that Arab thinkers will migrate in search of fresh air and to escape the sword of the religious authorities.[4]

The next three cases I will cite all come from Bangladesh. On 26 February 2015, Avijit Roy, a Bangladeshi-American activist and blogger, described as someone who "sought enlightenment in doubt, criticism and reason," was brutally hacked to death by Muslim extremists because of his writings that were critical of religion, especially Islam.[5] A little over a month later on 30 March 2015, a similar fate befell another Bangladeshi blogger, Washiqur Rahman, who was killed by fanatical Muslims for his criticisms of irrational religious beliefs and religious fundamentalism.[6] Less than two months after Rahman's killing, the life of yet another Bangladeshi blogger, Ananta Bijoy Das, was taken the same way on 12 May 2015 by Muslim fundamentalists for his writings championing science and criticizing Islamic (and other forms of religious) fundamentalism.[7] It is an unfortunate fact that such examples can be easily and quickly multiplied. Anyone who takes some time to investigate the occurrence of such incidents will soon see (if it is not already obvious to them) that they do occur with distressing regularity.

In my estimation, what Voltaire says about incidents of religiously motivated persecution carried out by Christians applies with at least as much force to Islam. "It is true that these absurd horrors do not stain the face of the earth every day," he says, "but they are frequent, and could easily fill a volume much greater than the gospels which condemn them."[8] Now, in considering the sorts of cases that I have cited, two initial responses may be proffered.

First, it may be argued that, strictly speaking, it is not *religious doubt* that invokes the wrath of religious fanatics, but rather other connected offences such as *questioning religious beliefs and practices, criticizing the religious government, religious mockery, apostasy,* etc. Although it is true that religious doubt does not always explicitly feature in the sorts of cases that I have mentioned, it is certainly referenced frequently enough to invite attention. Moreover, religious doubt does appear to be concomitant with things like questioning religious beliefs and practices, criticizing religious governments, etc., even if it is distinct from them. To see this, note how religious doubt sometimes leads to certain actions, like questioning religious beliefs and practices, and how it sometimes follows from

114 *Religious doubt and the Skeptical Muslim*

them. For instance, a Muslim who starts having doubts about whether the Qur'an is indeed revelation from God may be led to questioning this fundamental Islamic belief. Or, a Muslim who, say, is curious about the rational foundation of the Islamic belief in the Qur'an as God's Revelation and questions it may start doubting this belief, upon finding no rationally compelling arguments in support of it. Furthermore, in many cases involving religiously motivated persecution, the persecutors will often use terms like 'questioning', 'doubting', 'criticizing', 'rejecting', 'mocking', etc., interchangeably in their accusations, as though these are all synonyms for a single offense that allegedly follows from any critical discussion of Islamic belief. Getting clear about the nature of religious doubt should help in making clear that conflating it with these other terms is simply a mistake.

Second, it may also be argued that it is not the presence of religious doubt by itself that creates trouble, but rather the conjunction of such doubt *along with some principles of practice regarding what it to be done with religious doubters*; these practical principles may call for religious doubters to be punished, executed, etc. So, the argument may run, the main problem in the sorts of cases that I have cited concerns practical principles that call for religious doubters to be persecuted in some manner and not religious doubt *per se*. While I accept the point that there is indeed a difference between the presence of religious doubt and principles regarding what it is to be done with religious doubters (as there is a difference, for example, between the presence of pornography in a society and principles regarding what, if anything, is to be done with those who view pornographic material), I do not think this point suffices to take the focus away from religious doubt in the sorts of cases involving religiously motivated persecution that I have cited. For one thing, these principles of practice still mention religious doubt. Moreover, the call to action against religious doubters is mandated by such principles precisely because *religious doubt is seen as a bad thing*.

So, what *is* the problem with religious doubt, such that it is seen as incompatible with Islamic faith? In what follows, I will defend the thesis that religious doubt and Islamic faith are *compatible*. My discussion will proceed as follows: first, I will present a general understanding of what I take doubt to be. Next, I shall offer an account of how I shall construe religious doubt specifically and will describe the sort of religious doubter who is seen as a qualifying candidate for excommunication from the Muslim community. Following this, I will present and criticize a number of standard Islamic arguments for the incompatibility of religious doubt and Islamic faith. I shall argue that none of these arguments are successful. Given the failure of these arguments, it remains an open question whether a religious doubter should be excommunicated from the Muslim community. Finally, I will offer some considerations for the view that religious doubters should have a place within the Muslim community.

2. Religious doubt and the Skeptical Muslim – a preliminary analysis

2.1 An account of doubt in general

Doubt, as I understand it, is a kind of propositional attitude; more specifically, doubting a proposition, p, entails that one neither believes that p nor disbelieves that p. This seems to be the core understanding of doubt held by many philosophers. As Michael Williams writes, "Doubt is often defined as a state of indecision or hesitancy with respect to accepting or rejecting a proposition. Thus, doubt is opposed to belief."[9] Similarly, C. J. Hookway explains that "[w]hen we doubt a proposition, we neither believe nor disbelieve it: rather, we suspend judgement, regarding it as an open question whether it is true."[10] From this, it also follows that doubting a proposition p is opposed to holding the belief that p with (psychological) certainty, since doubt is opposed to belief *simpliciter*. A belief is psychologically certain, as Barry Reed characterizes it, "when the subject who has it is supremely convinced of its truth."[11]

Here, it may be suggested that, even if it is opposed to holding a belief with *certainty*, doubt is nevertheless compatible with holding beliefs that we are less than certain about. As Descartes showed using his Method of Doubt, various 'commonsensical' beliefs can be doubted when examined from the perspective of what Bernard Williams calls "the project of Pure Enquiry."[12] To consider one example that many philosophers have discussed, I believe with a strong degree of confidence that there exists a world that is external to my senses. But since I acknowledge the possibility of being deceived about this belief by the evil demon as envisaged by Descartes, does it not follow that that my belief in the existence of an external world is also something that I doubt? Not really, if we are talking about *genuine* doubt. The mere *possibility* that the evil demon may be deceiving me, as Hookway rightly observes, "does not touch my everyday confidence that I will be supported when I sit down." Although Descartes arguments may in a theoretical sense lead to *hyperbolic* doubt within the project of Pure Enquiry, such doubt does not appear to play any rational role in ordinary life.[13] For the purposes of my discussion in this chapter, my focus will be on genuine as opposed to hyperbolic doubt. Genuine doubt does appear to be incompatible with belief in relation to any given proposition (i.e., genuinely doubting the truth of a proposition, p, is incompatible with also believing that p). Henceforth, unless otherwise stated, all references to doubt will be to genuine doubt.

The incompatibility of doubt and belief can be further supported by considering Charles Peirce's helpful discussion of these two states of mind in his essay 'The Fixation of Belief'.[14] In this essay, Peirce distinguishes doubt from belief in a few ways. There are at least two relevant differences that I think he is correct to point out. First, there is a *practical* difference between

116 *Religious doubt and the Skeptical Muslim*

doubt and belief. Beliefs typically influence what we do, as in the following example Peirce provides:

> The Assassins, or followers of the Old Man of the Mountain, used to rush into death at his least command, because they believed that obedience to him would insure everlasting felicity. Had they doubted this, they would not have acted as they did.[15]

This is not to say that doubting the truth of a proposition instead of believing it will necessarily yield *no* practical effect, but rather that the practical effects will not be similar. This point applies more generally to believing in the truth of a proposition as opposed to doubting it. Second, there is this *cognitive* difference between doubt and belief:

> Doubt is an uneasy and dissatisfied state from which we struggle to free ourselves and pass into the state of belief; while the latter is a calm and satisfactory state which we do not wish to avoid, or to change to a belief in anything else.[16]

Peirce's point here appears right when we test it with some concrete examples. Think for a moment about the cognitive difference between doubting that your wife is faithful and believing that she is, between doubting that you will pass the exam and believing that you will or between doubting that you have your car keys with you and believing that you do.

Once in doubt about a given proposition, a person will "struggle to attain a state of belief," as Peirce puts it.[17] If the transition from doubt to belief is successful (i.e., when a person goes from a state of doubting that *p* to the belief that *p* or the belief that not-*p*), then the doubt has been *resolved*, as I will call it. By contrast, the persisting state of struggling to go from doubt to belief I will call *unresolved* doubt. Unresolved doubt can be *short term* in its duration. Consider, for instance, the situation where you find yourself doubting whether you left the stove turned on while you are shaving in the bathroom. A quick visit to the kitchen will speedily resolve the doubt, either when you find out (and come to believe) that the stove was indeed left turned on or else when you discover (and come to believe) that the stove was not left turned on. In other cases, unresolved doubt can have a *long-term* existence. One tragic example of this is the well-known case involving Madeleine McCann, who mysteriously disappeared from her bed in a holiday apartment on 3 May 2007. To this date, as I write this, her parents and many who took an interest in the case continue to have doubts about what really happened to Madeleine, because no plausible account of her disappearance has yet been offered.[18] Unresolved doubt may be long term – indeed, *indefinitely* long term – because present circumstances make it difficult if not (practically) impossible to resolve the truth of the proposition that one is doubting.[19]

The fact that, sometimes, attempting to eliminate or alleviate unresolved doubt is difficult, if not impossible, reveals one last point about doubt that is important for my subsequent discussion and argument. Like belief, doubt is not *directly* under our control. One cannot simply *choose* to start doubting the truth of a particular proposition or stop doubting it. Consider how you cannot simply start doubting whether the text that you are reading right now appears the right side up or stop doubting whether I have previously used the word 'commonsensical' in this book (now that I have drawn your attention to the matter). We do, however, sometimes have *indirect* control over doubt (as with belief). For example, a man may follow up on a friend's suggestion to investigate allegations regarding his wife's infidelity. Upon discovering incriminating evidence, such as text messages and racy photos on his wife's phone, he *then* doubts her fidelity. Similarly, a man who doubts his wife's faithfulness cannot simply 'switch off' the doubt; rather, he will try to investigate the matter in order to settle the question whether his wife is cheating on him or not. It is through our *actions* that doubt may arise or be resolved.

2.2 Religious doubt and the Skeptical Muslim

By *religious doubt*, I mean a certain *kind* of doubt, the basic aspects of which have been explained in the preceding section. Specifically, religious doubt is doubt regarding the truth of *religious* propositions, such as 'There is a God' or 'God will resurrect us all after death'. The sort of religious doubt that I am primarily interested in is doubt regarding the truth of what are regarded, from the perspective of a traditional Muslim theist, as *significant* religious propositions, as opposed to those that are *trivial*. Some examples of significant religious propositions are 'God exists', 'Muhammad is a Prophet of God' and 'The Qur'an is the inerrant Word of God'. By contrast, examples of trivial religious propositions would include some over which the four schools of (Sunni) Islamic jurisprudence disagree, such as 'It is forbidden for a Muslim man to shave his beard' or 'A Muslim woman must wear socks during prayer'. The significance of religious propositions is, in traditional Islam, determined in part by whether not believing in their truth puts one outside the fold of the faith. For this reason, many Muslims maintain that a person in the Muslim community who stops believing that Muhammad is a Prophet of God is no longer a Muslim. But, if all such a person did was not believe that Muslim women are required to wear socks during prayer, this alone would not be enough to disqualify him or her from being regarded as a Muslim.

Traditional Muslims are generally in agreement over what the significant religious propositions are around which their faith is built. Certainly, these would include belief in the existence of God and the Prophethood of Muhammad. In what follows, my focus will be on the 'Skeptical Muslim', who I shall take to be any person who satisfies the following *necessary* conditions – (1) identifies as a Muslim and (2) doubts the existence of God and/or the Prophethood of Muhammad.[20]

118 *Religious doubt and the Skeptical Muslim*

3. An evaluation of some arguments for the incompatibility of religious doubt and Islamic faith

3.1 The argument from the incoherence of the concept of the Skeptical Muslim

Here is one sort of argument that can be given against the very coherence of the concept of the 'Skeptical Muslim', someone who doubts the existence of God and/or the Prophethood of Muhammad. Religious *beliefs*, one might argue, are what we use to distinguish members of a religious community from those who are outside of that community. What separates Christians from non-Christians, for instance, are specific beliefs that those who identify as Christians hold about Jesus being the Son of God, the second person of the Trinity, the Savior of humanity, etc. If, however, religious beliefs are eschewed in discussions of religious identity, what is it that separates the doubting *Muslim* from a *non-Muslim* who doubts the truth of Islamic belief? It looks as though the position of the 'Skeptical Muslim' amounts to saying that one is both a Muslim and a non-Muslim, which is absurd.

Reply: The problem with this argument is that it falsely assumes religious beliefs constitute a necessary condition for religious identification. A person may choose to identify as a Muslim not because he believes that Islamic doctrine is true but because he relates to, and may even participate in, Islamic *practice*. Ali A. Rizvi explains how the distinction between Islamic belief and practice applied in his own case of religious identification as a Muslim:

> [T]ry to imagine divorcing the ideas in your religion from the person that you are, or the community you belong to. Are you able to see a distinction between Islamic ideology and Muslim identity? Suppose someone told you could keep your family and community traditions, enjoy the feasts of Ramadan, and celebrate the Eid holidays with family and friends like always — but without the burden of defending every line in your scripture. Would you consider it? I did. And today, I enjoy the Muslim experience much more without the burden of having to believe in Islam.[21]

But, one might object, what could possibly *motivate* such a commitment to the religious experience if no beliefs are involved? In response to such a question, several philosophers have suggested *pragmatic* considerations as an alternative source of motivation for religious commitment. Richard Swinburne, for instance, has defended the viability of what he calls the 'Pragmatist view' of faith. On this model of faith, one essentially *acts as if* he has religious beliefs.[22] Commenting specifically on the applicability of this view of faith to Christian commitment, Swinburne writes:

> [O]n the Pragmatist view, a person has Christian faith if he acts on the assumption that there is a God who has the properties which Christians

Religious doubt and the Skeptical Muslim   119

ascribe to him and seeks to do those good actions which the love of God (if there is a God) would lead him to do ... The person of Pragmatist faith ... prays for his brethren, not necessarily because he believes that there is a God who hears his prayers, but because there is a chance that there is a God who will hear those prayers and help his brethren. He worships not necessarily because he believes that there is a God who deserves worship, but because it is very important to express gratitude if there is a God to whom to be grateful, and there is some chance that there is.[23]

The Skeptical Muslim may be in a state of doubt because he thinks that the evidence for belief in the existence of God and/or the Prophethood of Muhammad is insufficient. But this assessment of the evidential support for Islamic belief is compatible with non-doxastic propositional attitudes, such as acceptance or hope.[24]

3.2 The Argument from the Nonexistence of Skeptical Muslims

Another sort of argument that can be given against religious doubt and the notion of a 'Skeptical Muslim' is that such things do not exist. That is, there is no, nor can there _really_ be, any religious doubt about Islam. What this must mean is that the idea of a 'Skeptical Muslim', even if coherent, is simply a myth, much like the centaur or hydra. There are no Skeptical Muslims. Individuals who claim to be doubting Muslims are just wrong about identifying their state as one of _religious doubt_. The following analogy may serve to clarify the line of thought here. Suppose one thought (rightly or wrongly) that there simply is no such thing as 'love at first sight'. Because of this, a person would regard those who _claim_ to have fallen in love at first sight to be wrong about this; perhaps these individuals confused sexual attraction or some other feeling with love. In a similar vein, those who defend The Argument from the Nonexistence of Skeptical Muslims claim that Muslims who profess to have religious doubts about Islam are mistaken. Such people are _lying_ and in _denial_, much like the drug addict or alcoholic who refuses to admit that he or she has a problem even though evidence to the contrary is overwhelming and attests to an obvious truth. Essentially, the thought here is that the evidence supporting Islamic belief is so clear and abundant that claims to doubt Islamic belief are just _denials_ of what is apparent to everyone, Muslim or otherwise. Commenting specifically on the knowledge of God, the Shi'ite thinker Ayatollah Abdul Husayn Dastaghaib Shirazi states the following in his _Qalbe-Saleem_ ('Immaculate Conscience'):

The ... excuse of one who does not know Allah and is unaware of Him, is not acceptable ... Allah is not hidden from any sensible person ... whatever is present in the universe are all proofs of His Absolute

120 *Religious doubt and the Skeptical Muslim*

Knowledge, Wisdom, Power and Command. Hence there is a Being, infinitely knowledgeable and Wise, Omniscient, Mighty, Omnipotent, and Powerful ... People, who doubt, are in fact those who do not want to recognize the truth itself. If they were really seekers of truth, they would have had looked at the creatures of the world and sought a lesson from it. If they had looked at the marvel of the wisdom and amazing power of the Creator of the Universe with proper attention, they would never have doubted.[25]

Here, Shirazi addresses only the knowledge of God in a general sense and does not say anything further about evidence that would distinguish Islam from other theistic religions, such as Judaism and Christianity. What about the evidence in support of the Muslim belief that Muhammad is a Prophet of God, for instance? On this matter, Shaykh 'Abdul Rahman 'Abdul Khaliq expresses his view as follows:

My brothers and sisters everywhere! You should know that the Messenger, Muhammad the son of 'Abdullah (may Allah's blessings and peace be upon him) is Allah's Messenger in reality and truth. The evidences that show his veracity are abundant. None but an infidel, who out of arrogance alone, could deny these signs.[26]

What this means is that any person who does not acknowledge the *shahada* ('There is no god but Allah and Muhammad is The Messenger of Allah') is like a person who refuses to acknowledge the conjunctive proposition 'People exist and some people who have existed were women'. So-called 'Skeptical Muslims', and indeed anyone who claims to have religious doubts about Islam, must be lying.

Reply: This argument hinges on the claim that the evidence for Islamic belief is so overwhelming and undeniable that it excludes all possible cases of genuine doubt about Islam. While it is understandable that a traditionalist Muslim would hold this view, the real question is whether this is indeed the case. As I have noted in the previous chapter, however, it is far from clear that belief in the existence of God and the Prophethood of Muhammad can be supported by evidence and argument. Until and unless a proponent of The Argument from the Nonexistence of Skeptical Muslims can provide rationally compelling evidence for God's existence and Muhammad's Prophethood, this particular argument fails.

3.3 The Argument from Belief with Certainty

A fairly common argument against the compatibility of religious doubt and Islamic faith, and hence against the notion of a 'Skeptical Muslim', appeals to holding religious belief with certainty as a requirement for being a Muslim. Since the Skeptical Muslim is, by definition, someone who harbors

Religious doubt and the Skeptical Muslim   121

doubts about Islamic belief, he or she cannot really be regarded as a Muslim. Sheikh Muhammed Salih Al-Munajjid explains the view that constitutes a critical premise in this argument as follows:

> The kufr [denial of faith] of doubt ... means hesitating with regard to following the truth and being uncertain as to whether it is true, because what is required is certainty of faith (yaqeen) that what the Messenger [i.e., Muhammad] brought is truth with no hint of doubt in it. Whoever thinks that what he brought may not be true has disbelieved, in the sense of kufr of doubt.[27]

Reply: The trouble with this argument is that one of its critical premises, the claim that holding religious belief with certainty is a requirement for being a Muslim, is just not plausible. The first thing to note is that it is a matter of dispute among Muslim exegetes whether the Qur'an supports such a view. One can find some verses that appear to suggest that the Muslim faithful must believe with certainty. For instance, Qur'an 2:4 describes the believers are those "who believe in what has been revealed to you, [O Muhammad], and what was revealed before you, and of the Hereafter they are certain [in faith]." And again, in Qur'an 51:20, we read that "on earth are signs for the certain [in faith]." Other verses, however, appear to support the view that religious belief can exist without certainty because faith is something that can increase. For instance, Qur'an 8:2 says: "The believers are only those who, when Allah is mentioned, their hearts become fearful, and when His verses are recited to them, it increases them in faith; and upon their Lord they rely." And Qur'an 48:4 says: "It is He who sent down tranquility into the hearts of the believers that they would increase in faith along with their [present] faith."

A second problem with the argument is that, if taken seriously, it would mean that a good number of professing *Muslims*, perhaps even the majority, must be regarded as unbelievers. The reason for this is that, despite what someone like Sheikh Al-Munajjid might say, most Muslims probably do not hold their religious beliefs with certainty. As Andrew Chignell notes in his assessment of Alvin Plantinga's religious epistemology, according to which faith constitutes knowledge:

> [B]y placing the focus largely on knowledge, Plantinga valorizes an ideal which only a select group of people will be able to realize, at least in the *ante-mortem* ... Perhaps there are epistemic saints among us who don't struggle with unbelief—maybe they consistently hold their religious beliefs with the degree of strength sufficient for knowledge. And perhaps there are moments when an average theist is overwhelmingly aware of God's presence such that all shadow of doubt flees and the propositions which she once took on faith are held firmly enough to achieve the status of knowledge. But I suspect that the vast majority of believers, most of the time, will have to settle for something considerably less exalted.[28]

122   *Religious doubt and the Skeptical Muslim*

It is interesting to note that a Muslim like Al-Ash'ari didn't have a problem with this view, declaring a *muqallid*, an adherent of *taqlid* (imitation), to be an unbeliever as his or her faith is not based on intellectual arguments.[29] Since most Muslims base their faith on *taqlid* and not intellectual arguments, the consequence of taking al-Ash'ari's view seriously is that the Muslim masses are guilty of unbelief. Avoiding this problematic consequence means dropping the requirement of holding religious beliefs with certainty before one can be regarded as a Muslim. But in doing this, one can no longer use The Argument from Belief with Certainty against Skeptical Muslims.

3.4 *The argument from belief*

In response to the criticisms of the previous argument, one might modify The Argument from Belief with Certainty by simply dropping the certainty requirement. In doing so, we have The Argument from Belief, according to which a Muslim is someone who *believes* that God exists and that Muhammad is His Messenger. As the Qur'an states:

> The Messenger has believed in what was revealed to him from his Lord, and [so have] the believers. All of them have believed in Allah and His angels and His books and His messengers, [saying], 'We make no distinction between any of His messengers.' And they say, 'We hear and we obey. [We seek] Your forgiveness, our Lord, and to You is the [final] destination.'
>
> (2:285)

Since the Skeptical Muslim does not believe these things, he or she cannot be regarded as a Muslim.

Reply: One problem with this argument is that it glosses over two important senses of 'belief', belief-that and belief-in; believing *that* God exists refers to having a doxastic attitude towards the proposition 'God exists', whereas believing *in* God refers to trusting in God.[30] The Qur'anic reference to *iman* is often translated as 'faith' or 'belief'. *Iman* comes from the verb *amana*, which means 'to be secure' or 'to put trust in' something. Having faith (*iman*) in God is to trust in God, His commandments, etc.; thus understood, Islamic faith refers to belief *in* God and not (just) the belief *that* God exists. Believing that God exists does not automatically mean that one believes in God. Satan (*Iblis*) clearly believes that God exists (Satan is no atheist) but does not believe in God (i.e., he does not have faith or *iman*). Based on this brief analysis, it seems that the locus of faith is not mere belief-that. If this is correct, then perhaps a sort of skeptical faith is a viable option for the doubting Muslim, where religious beliefs are not required. I have already noted this possibility in responding to the argument from the incoherence of the concept of The Skeptical Muslim (see 3.1 above).

3.5 The argument from disbelief (Kufr)

One final argument for the incompatibility of religious doubt and Islamic faith that I will consider here appeals to the Islamic understanding of disbelief (*kufr*). It might be argued that the Skeptical Muslim, because of his or doubts, is guilty of disbelief (*kufr*). And, the argument may continue, the Qur'an neither speaks favorably of *kufr* nor in any way identifies it with Muslims who have *iman*. Hence, there can be no such individual as the Skeptical Muslim, seeing that such an individual would be guilty of *kufr* – the very antithesis of *iman*.

Reply: This argument fails in showing that religious doubt and Islamic faith are incompatible because it commits a category mistake in applying the label of *kufr* to religious doubt. *Kufr* is the exact opposite of *iman*. Literally, the word means 'to conceal' or 'to cover up' something. In a Qur'anic context, it refers to covering up or concealing religious truth. The person guilty of *kufr* – the *kafir* – intentionally covers up that which he or she knows is true. As Wilfred Cantwell Smith writes:

> *Kufr* (so-called 'infidelity'), the heinous sin, the incomprehensibly stupid and perverse obduracy, is not unbelief but 'refusal'. It is almost a spitting in God's face when He speaks out of His infinite authority and vast compassion. It is man's dramatic negative response to this spectacular divine initiative.[31]

Smith's understanding of *kufr* is shared by many other commentators of the Qur'an. For instance, Abdullah Yusuf Ali, whose English translation of the Qur'an is perhaps the most widely read, explains: "*Kafara, kufr, kāfir*, and derivate forms of the word, imply a deliberate rejection of Faith as opposed to a mistaken idea of Allah or faith, which is not inconsistent with an earnest desire to seek the truth."[32] In another (Shi'ite) commentary on the Qur'an, the authors explain the notion of *kufr* as follows:

> Philologically, the term ... kufr ... means 'to cover, to conceal'. In religion it means: 'to deny the Grace or the Existence of Allah, His prophet, the prophecies of the apostles, and the Resurrection'. He who denies these principles of the religion, even only one of them, according to the consensus of Muslims, is out of the Circle of Islam and becomes counted among the disbelievers.[33]

Although the *kafir* rejects God and lacks faith in Him, he nevertheless *knows* – and therefore *believes* – that there is a God, that God's commandments are to be obeyed, etc. Now, since the Skeptical Muslim is by definition someone who doubts – and therefore does *not believe* – that there is a God, that God's commandments are to be obeyed, etc., one cannot regard such a person as a *kafir*.

124   *Religious doubt and the Skeptical Muslim*

4. Some concluding remarks about religious doubt, Islamic faith and the Skeptical Muslim

In this chapter, I explored several arguments that can be given against the compatibility of religious doubt and Islamic faith and found them wanting. None of these arguments succeed in showing that the idea of a 'Skeptical Muslim' does not make sense or that there is a rational basis for shunning or excluding such a person from the Muslim community. In my concluding remarks for this chapter and the book, I want to end with a brief positive case in defense of Skeptical Muslims to supplement my criticism of the arguments discussed in this chapter. As noted earlier, some cases of doubt may end up being resolved. A person who is a Skeptical Muslim need not be seen as someone who is permanently situated in that state. Perhaps his or her doubts will eventually be resolved by philosophical reflection on religious matters, by participation in the Muslim community, etc. The point about doubt not being directly under our control is an important one to keep in mind for those who are critical of the Skeptical Muslim's religious doubt. For, the Skeptical Muslim might protest, how can he or she simply 'switch off' the doubt and directly acquire Islamic *belief* (another mental state that is not directly under our control)? If ought implies can – a principle that is not unreasonable from a Qur'anic point of view (see, for example, 2:286) – the imperative to 'stop doubting and start believing' mistakenly presupposes that doubting and believing are actions and that one has the direct ability to do one and refrain from the other. It might be replied that one has *indirect* control over doubt and belief and that the Skeptical Muslim should *act as if* he or she believes until belief is acquired. But more needs to be said here if this insistence is to be regarded as anything more than urging the religious doubter to 'fake it until you make it'. Moreover, as noted earlier, the locus of Islamic faith is not belief-that but rather belief-in. It also needs to be asked why doubt about religious matters must be regarded as a *bad* thing. Arguably, sincere doubt requires a respectful attitude towards the truth; the sincere doubter cares for the truth and wants to ensure that he or she believes things that are true and avoids believing things that are false. It is this commitment to the truth that creates doubt. No traditional Muslim can argue that care for the truth is unimportant in Islam. Consider how Islamic thought is deeply concerned with the *truth* of religious belief, for example, in its constant warning against idolatry, worship of something other than the true God. This point can be further emphasized. One of God's Names in Islam is 'The Truth' (6:62). God commands His people that they should "cover not truth with falsehood, nor conceal the truth when [they] know (what it is)" (2:42). We are told that the truth is from God (2:147) and that the Word of God finds its fulfillment in truth (6:115). On the Day of Judgment, "[t]he truthful will profit from their truth" (5:119). It is perhaps for these reasons that one finds certain Prophetic traditions in which doubt is paradoxically regarded as a sign of faith. There is, for instance, the following *hadith*

Religious doubt and the Skeptical Muslim   125

in which some commentators state that the reference to 'thoughts which we cannot dare talk about' is a reference to religious doubt:

> Abu Hurairah said; His companion came to him and said; Messenger of Allah! We have thoughts which we cannot dare talk about and we do not like that we have them or talk about them. He said: Have you experienced that? They replied: yes. He said: that is clear faith.[34]

Perhaps, then, religious faith and religious doubt are not as far apart as one might think, even though one is generally extolled and the other generally disparaged.[35]

Notes

1 'For seeking answers on Islam, Muslim gets charged with blasphemy', www.themalaymailonline.com/malaysia/article/for-asking-questions-muslim-gets-charged-with-blasphemy.
2 'When asking questions is dangerous', www.themalaymailonline.com/opinion/zurairi-ar/article/when-asking-questions-is-dangerous.
3 'The Writings of Saudi Blogger Raif Badawi', www.huffingtonpost.com/stephen-schwartz/the-writings-of-saudi-blo_b_7733176.html.
4 'A look at the writings of Saudi blogger Raif Badawi – sentenced to 1,000 lashes', www.theguardian.com/world/2015/jan/14/-sp-saudi-blogger-extracts-raif-badawi.
5 'American writer hacked to death in Bangladesh spoke out against extremists', http://edition.cnn.com/2015/02/28/asia/bangladeshi-american-blogger-dead/.
6 'Knife attack kills Bangladesh blogger Washiqur Rahman', www.bbc.com/news/world-asia-32112433.
7 'Ananta Bijoy Das: Yet another Bangladeshi blogger hacked to death', http://edition.cnn.com/2015/05/12/asia/bangladesh-blogger-killed/.
8 Voltaire, 'Treatise on Tolerance', www.constitution.org/volt/tolerance.htm.
9 Michael Williams, 'Doubt', in Edward Craig (ed.), *The Shorter Routledge Encyclopedia of Philosophy*, (New York: Routledge, 2005), p. 199.
10 C. J. Hookway, 'Doubt', in Ted Honderich (ed.), *The Oxford Companion to Philosophy*, Second Edition, (Oxford: Oxford University Press, 2005), p. 220.
11 Barry Reed, 'Certainty', *The Stanford Encyclopedia of Philosophy* (Winter 2011 Edition), Edward N. Zalta (ed.), http://plato.stanford.edu/archives/win2011/entries/certainty/.
12 Bernard Williams, *Descartes: The Project of Pure Enquiry*, (Abingdon: Routledge, 2005).
13 Ibid., p. 46.
14 Charles S. Peirce, 'The Fixation of Belief', Popular Science Monthly 12 (November 1877), 1–15. www.peirce.org/writings/p107.html.
15 Ibid.
16 Ibid.
17 Ibid.
18 'Why we're still obsessed with the disappearance of Madeleine McCann', www.news.com.au/lifestyle/real-life/news-life/why-were-still-obsessed-with-the-disappearance-of-madeleine-mccann/news-story/962056cbe6d95cc5a85e36f027803484.
19 The precise demarcation point (if there is one) between 'short-term' and 'long-term' doubt is not important for the discussion that follows. The main

126 *Religious doubt and the Skeptical Muslim*

thing to note is that unresolved doubt can exist for long, and indeed indefinite, period.

20 That these conditions are only necessary but not sufficient will become clear below.

21 Ali A. Rizvi, 'On Belief vs. Identity: Letter to a Young North American Muslim', www.huffingtonpost.com/ali-a-rizvi/on-belief-identity-a-lett_b_7701278.html.

22 Richard Swinburne, *Faith and Reason*, Second Edition, (Oxford: Oxford University Press, 2005), p. 147.

23 Ibid., p. 148.

24 See William P. Alston, 'Belief, Acceptance, and Religious Faith', in J. Jordan and D. Howard-Snyder (eds.), *Faith, Freedom, and Rationality: Philosophy of Religion Today*, (London: Rowman & Littlefield, 1996) and Louis Pojman, 'Faith, Doubt and Belief, or Does Faith Entail Belief?' in R. M. Gale and A. R. Pruss (eds.), *The Existence of God*, (Aldershot and Burlington: Ashgate, 2003).

25 Ayatollah Abdul Husayn Dastaghaib Shirazi, *Immaculate Conscience*, available online at: www.al-islam.org/qalbe-saleem-immaculate-conscience-ayatullah-sayyid-abdul-husayn-dastghaib-shirazi/fourth-disease.

26 Shaykh 'Abdul Rahman 'Abdul Khaliq, 'Twelve Proofs that Muhammad is a True Prophet', www.saaid.net/islam/8.htm (last accessed 3/31/2015).

27 Sheikh Muhammed Salih Al-Munajjid, 'Kufr and its various kinds', Islam Question and Answer, http://islamqa.info/en/21249.

28 Andrew Chignell, 'Epistemology for Saints', www.booksandculture.com/articles/2002/marapr/10.20.html?paging=off.

29 Jeffry R. Halverson, *Theology and Creed in Sunni Islam*, (New York: Palgrave Macmillan, 2010), pp. 21–22.

30 For further discussion, see Paul Helm, *Faith with Reason*, (Oxford: Oxford University Press, 2000), pp. 103–111.

31 Wilfred Cantwell Smith, 'Faith, in the Qur'ān; and Its Relation to Belief', in his *On Understanding Islam*, (Mouton Publishers, 1981), p. 123.

32 Abdullah Yusuf Ali, *The Holy Qur'an: English translation of the meanings and Commentary*, revised and edited, (Medina, Saudi Arabia: King Fahd Holy Qur'an Printing Complex, n.d.), p. 8, note 30.

33 Sayyid Abbas Sadr-'ameli, trans., *An Enlightening Commentary into the Light of the Holy Qur'an vol. 1*, www.al-islam.org/enlightening-commentary-light-holy-quran-vol-1/section-1#disbelievers-second-group.

34 Sunan Abi Dawud 5110, https://sunnah.com/abudawud/43.

35 For an interesting historical treatment of skepticism and doubt in Islam, see Paul Heck, *Skepticism in Classical Islam: Moments of Confusion*, (New York, NY: Routledge, 2014).

Index

Abrahamov, Binyamin 2
Abu Hanifah 3
'Abd al-Jabbar 4, 31–32
Adams, Robert 64
Akhtar, Shabbir 1, 10, 82, 107
Al-Ash'ari 5–8, 14, 122
Al-Baghdadi 9
Al-Baqillani 9
Al-Farabi 10, 14, 47
Al-Ghazali 9; assessment of his
    scholastic fideism 35–71
Al-Hasan al-Basri 3
Al-Harawi, 'Abd Allah al-Ansari 3
Al-Juwayni 9
Al-Kindi x
Al-Ma'mun 4
Al-Mutawakkil 5
Al-Shafi'i 3, 16
Ali, Abdullah Yusuf 123
Alston, William P. 106
Amesbury, Richard x
Asad, Muhammad 83
Audi, Robert 58
Ayer, A.J. 65

Barth, Karl 77, 107
Boullata, Issa J. 103

Chignell, Andrew 121
Craig, William Lane 102
Cragg, Kenneth 81

Davis, Stephen T. 100–101
Demant, Peter R. 85
doubt: a general account 115–117;
    religious 117–125; about Islamic
    belief 112–114; arguments for the
    incompatibility of religious doubt and
    Islamic faith 118–125

Euben, Roxanne L. 85, 86
evil: problem of 107–108

faith and reason in Islam: a brief history
    2–10
fideism: as an obstacle to a
    philosophical investigation of Islam
    1; anti-rationalistic fideism ix, 2;
    traditionalist fideism ix, 2; scholastic
    fideism ix, 2; classical traditionalist
    fideism in Islam 14–33; classical
    scholastic fideism in Islam 35–71;
    contemporary fideism in Islam 76–96
Frank, Richard M. 36

Gimaret, D. 4

Hick, John 28
historical criticism: challenge of
    106–107
Hookway, C.J. 115

Ibn Hanbal 3, 4–5, 108
Ibn Khaldun 1, 8–9
Ibn Qudama 3; assessment of his
    traditionalist fideism 14–33
Ibn Rushd 10, 24, 28, 36, 104
Ibn Sina 10, 14, 47
Ibn Taymiyyah 3
Ibrahim al-Nazzam 25
Islam: moral objection to Islamic belief
    108–109

James, William 62

kalam 4; Ash'arite understanding of
    6–9
Keller, Nu Ha Mim 76
Khalidi, Muhammad Ali 45, 46

128 *Index*

Khundmiri, Alam 71
Kierkegaard, Soren 77
Küng, Hans 107

Mackie, J.L. 101
Makdisi, George 15, 35
Malik b. Anas 3
Marmura, Michael E. 35
Maududi, Abu A'la viii; Maududi's
    fideism 77–85
McCarthy, Richard 42, 67, 70
Menn, Stephen 50
Muslim: The Skeptical 117–125
Mu'tazilites 3–5

Nakamura, Kojiro 35
Nasr, Seyyed Hossein 106

Pascal, Blaise 62, 64
Peirce, Charles 115, 116
Peters, F.E. 9, 106
philosophy: definition of vii
philosophical investigation of Islam:
    why it is important viii–ix; whether it
    is possible 1–10
philosophy of religion: definition of vii
Plantinga, Alvin 121
Popkin, Richard vii
Pruss, Alexander 101

Qadhi, Yasir 76
Qutb, Sayyid: Qutb's fideism 85–96

Rahman, Fazlur x, 4
Ramsey, Frank viii
rationalist arguments: for Islamic
    belief 100–110; for God's existence
    100–103; for the Prophethood of
    Muhammad 103–104; prospects of
    105–109
Reed, Barry 115
religious diversity: problem of
    105–106
Rippin, Andrew 103, 104
Rizvi, Ali 118
Rowe, William 102
Russell, Bertrand 66

Schuon, Frithjof 105
Shirazi, Ayatollah Abdul Husayn
    Dastaghaib 119–120
Smith, Jane I. 59
Smith, Wilfred Cantwell 123
Stewart, David vii
Swinburne, Richard 65, 104, 109–110,
    118–119

Tertullian 15
theistic rationalism 2

Wasil ibn Ata 3
Watt, W. Montgomery 5, 6, 35, 41, 105
Williams, Bernard 115
Williams, Michael 115
Williams, Wesley 3